# BLACK BONDAGE

# BLACK BONDAGE

## THE LIFE OF SLAVES
## IN THE SOUTH

Walter Goodman

FARRAR, STRAUS & GIROUX

NEW YORK

*An Ariel Book*

# CONTENTS

Introduction: The Question     3

One: Arrival     5

Two: Work     17

Three: Play     42

Four: Punishment     63

Five: The Family     85

Six: Resistance     113

Epilogue: Freedom     143

Index     147

*Tisn't he who has stood and looked on that can tell you what slavery is—'tis he who has endured. . . . I was black, but I had the feelings of a man as well as any man.*

Benjamin Drew,
*The Refugee*

# NEGROES
## FOR SALE.

☞**Will be sold at public auction, at Spring Hill, in the County of Hempstead, on a credit of twelve months, on Fri day the 28th day of this present month, 15 young and valuable Slaves, consisting of 9 superior Men & Boys, between 12 and 27 years of age, one woman about 43 years who is** a good washer and cook, one woman about twenty-seven, and one very likely young woman with three children.

Also at the same time, and on the same terms, three Mules, about forty head of Cattle, plantation tools, one waggon, and a first rate Gin stand, manufactured by Pratt &Co.

Bond with two or more approved securities will be required.
Sale to commence at 10 o'clock.

*E. E. Hundley,*
*W. Robinson,*
*H. M. Robinson.*

Announcement of a slave auction

INTRODUCTION

# *THE QUESTION*

"Why am I a slave? Why are some people slaves and others masters? Was there ever a time when this was not so? How did the relation commence?"

Such were the questions that puzzled eight-year-old Frederick Douglass, who, born a slave in Maryland, escaped to the North at the age of twenty-one and devoted the remainder of his life to fighting for his people's rights.

Many other boys and girls, the children of those who labored under an overseer's whip in the cotton, tobacco, sugar, and rice fields of the South during the first half of the nineteenth century, must have asked themselves questions much like those posed by young Douglass, as it dawned on them that they were destined to work out their entire lives as the property of one white master or another.

It is more than a hundred years since Abraham Lincoln issued the Emancipation Proclamation that bestowed freedom on four million black Americans. But the experience of slavery still troubles America's conscience—as it must until its effects are eradicated, its injustices somehow redeemed.

The purpose of this book is to convey to young readers who received the prize of freedom as a birthright a sense of what it was like to be a slave on a plantation in the South around 1830–1850. If we do not at least try to understand that, then we cannot hope to understand what has happened between blacks and whites in this country in the century since the Civil War, what is happening today, what may happen tomorrow.

# ONE

# *ARRIVAL*

Many immigrants have come to these shores, from many parts of the globe, and it is one of our nation's proudest claims that they found opportunity here denied them in the lands of their birth. Most came eagerly, fleeing poverty and oppression in the Old World, with hope for a new start in the New World. For millions such hopes were realized, and they passed onto their children and their children's children a faith in America as a land of freedom and opportunity.

But the child born into slavery learned early that his was a different heritage. The journey of his parents or grandparents or great-grandparents to America was made not in high expectations but in chains. They did not come because they sought a better life for themselves but because other men found profit in bringing them here.

Their ordeal began in their native Africa, where slavery seems to have existed even before the arrival of the white man—but it was not until the opening up of the dark continent by Portuguese explorers that the export of human beings became a profitable business. Cheap labor was needed for the fields of the New World—the West Indies and the Americas—and, beginning in the sixteenth century, European vessels took to plying the African coast, offering merchandise in exchange for men, women, and children.

The traders did most of their business through tribal chieftains who would attack weaker tribes, burn their villages, and lead the survivors into captivity. For a handful of goods, a few muskets, they would deliver other Africans, and even their own people, into bondage. The guns that the obliging chieftains received from the Europeans enabled them to carry out their raids more efficiently, and so they were able to supply more and more slaves as the demand increased in the sixteenth and seventeenth centuries.

In some places, enterprising tribesmen would hide in the territory of another tribe, on the lookout for a child playing alone. When they saw one, they would gag him, tie his hands and feet, fling him over a shoulder, and bear him off like a sack of meal to where the slave trader waited; a healthy child might bring ten dollars' worth of cloth or beads or rum to his kidnapper. It was not unheard of, however, for the kidnappers themselves to be kidnapped, put in chains by the Europeans, and transported across the ocean along with their victims.

After being captured, the prisoners were marched to a trading center—a forced march of many miles usually, which brought pain to all and death to some. The victims were bound together in a human caravan, called a coffle, and driven along like animals through wild country where wild beasts preyed, with no shelter from the fierce African sun or battering rain. While their sale was being completed, they would most likely be penned in for a time at the trading center. Here at least they were protected from the elements by some sort of roof. Women and children were permitted to walk about as they pleased; the men were chained together and kept under armed guard.

In the process of being traded, every slave was carefully examined by the potential buyer—not out of any charitable interest in the black man's health but simply to avoid being cheated. Slave sellers early developed methods of making sick men look well and old men look young (by oiling their bodies, for example, and by shaving their heads so that no gray hairs showed), and the buyers had no wish to invest in second-rate merchandise.

Here are two contemporary descriptions of a flourishing African slave market in the 1850's:

"Near the middle of the square are groups of children, some not more than five years old, looking old already. They sit in silence or rise up when required, they utter few words amongst themselves, for they have long lost parents and friends and those in the same position sitting around them are utter strangers, often foreigners, to them."

"Fierce Arabs, Turks and Abyssinians are busy with their bargains. First lot, a row of little children of about five years, valued at two dollars. Second lot, girls of ten; price from five to ten dollars. Third, youths of nineteen, stout fellows worth from four to twelve dollars. Fourth, worn-out women and old men. These latter are sold cheaply, about a dollar each, being on their last legs. Nearly all are half asleep, their poor old heads dropping from sheer fatigue and their poor persecuted bodies as dry as a chip."

The healthy slave purchased for a few dollars' worth of merchandise in Africa might bring ten times his cost in the New World.

Once the sale was completed, the slave was branded with the mark of the buyer and was ready for the last part of his journey to the coast, where the slave ships lay at anchor. For people who had never been near the sea before, the first sight of what appeared to be a limitless body of water was terrifying. The roar of the surf and the crash of the breakers, the ship riding at anchor in the distance, waiting to take them away from the land where they were born and raised to a mysterious destination, the strange hairy faces of white sailors, who, for all the frightened Africans knew, were planning to eat them—all this so added to the captives' terror that some attempted suicide by jumping from the canoes as they were being rowed out to the waiting ship.

One ship's captain wrote:

"The Negroes are so wilful and loth to leave their own country, that they have often leap'd out of the canoes, boat and ship, into the sea, and kept under water till they were drowned, to avoid being taken up and saved by our boats, which pursued them. . . . We have likewise seen divers of them eaten by sharks, of which a prodigious number kept about the ships in this place. . . ."

Nothing about the slave ship was designed to reassure the people as to what was in store for them. An eleven-year-old boy, kidnapped in the African kingdom of Benin, later learned English and recorded his emotions on first boarding the vessel that would take him across the seas:

"When I looked round the ship and saw a large furnace of copper boiling and a multitude of black people of every description chained together, every one of their countenances expressing dejection or sorrow, I no longer doubted my fate, and quite overpowered with horror, I fell motionless on the deck and fainted. When I recovered a little, I found some black people about me. . . . I asked them if we were to be eaten by these white men with horrible looks, red faces and long hair."

In the early days of the slave trade, the people were simply thrown into the hold of the ship to survive as best they could the wait in the harbor, often for many weeks, while the human cargo was being gathered together, and then the long voyage across the Atlantic Ocean. So many did not survive the stifling heat and stench and accumulating filth that slavers took to housing their unwilling passengers on deck, in shelters made of branches and bamboo shoots. The hard, bare, splintery planks served as beds, and so jammed together were the captives on many ships that everyone had to sleep on his side, with no space even for rolling over.

A first-hand observer, an English minister, has left us a description of the conditions under which black people made the journey to the New World:

"The cargo of a vessel of a hundred tons or a little more is calculated to purchase from 220 to 250 slaves. Their lodging rooms below the deck, which are three (for the men, the boys and the women) besides a place for the sick, are sometimes more than five feet high and sometimes less, and this height is divided toward the

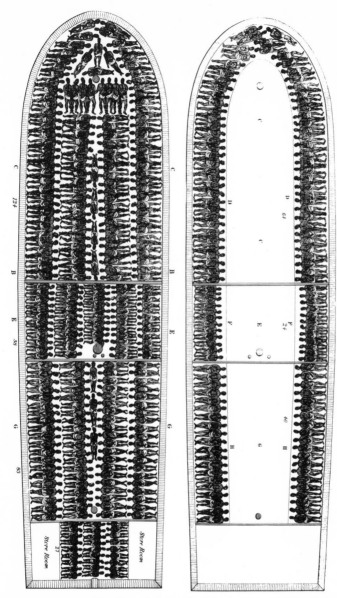

Loading plan for a slave ship, from an 1839 lithograph published in London

middle, for the slaves lie in two rows, one above the other, on each side of the ship, so close to each other like books on a shelf. I have known them so close that the shelf would not easily contain one more.

"The poor creatures, thus cramped, are likewise in irons for the most part which makes it difficult for them to turn or move or attempt to rise or to lie down without hurting themselves or each other. Every morning, perhaps, more instances than one are found of the living and the dead fastened together."

And here is the experience as seen by a young African who actually made the journey:

"At last, when the ship we were in had got in all her cargo, they made ready with many fearful noises, and we were all put under deck, so that we could not see how they managed the vessel.

"But this disappointment was the least of my sorrow. The stench of the hold while we were on the coast was so intolerably loathsome that it was dangerous to remain there for any time, and some of us had been permitted to stay on the deck for the fresh air; but now that the whole ship's cargo were confined together, it became absolutely pestilential.

"The closeness of the place, and the heat of the climate, added to the number in the ship, which was so crowded that each had scarcely room to turn himself, almost suffocated us. This produced copious perspirations, so that the air soon became unfit for respiration, from a variety of loathsome smells, and brought on a sickness among the slaves, of which many died. . . .

"This wretched situation was again aggravated by the galling of the chains, now become insupportable; and the filth of the necessary tubs, into which the children often fell and were almost suffocated. The shrieks of the women and the groans of the dying rendered the whole a scene of horror almost inconceivable."

In their book on the Atlantic slave trade, *Black Cargoes,* Daniel P. Mannix and Malcolm Cowley describe a typical day in mid-passage. Women and children were allowed to roam at large, but the men were attached by leg irons to chains that ran along the ship's bulwarks. After a breakfast of rice or cornmeal or yams, with perhaps a scrap of meat thrown in, and a little water, there came the ceremony of "dancing the slaves"—a compulsory form of exercise designed, it was said, for the captive's physical and mental well-being.

The authors picture the scene:

"While sailors paraded the deck, each with a cat-o'-nine tails in his right hand, the men slaves 'jumped in their irons' until their ankles were bleeding flesh. . . . Music was provided by a slave thumping on a broken drum or an upturned kettle or by an African banjo, if there was one aboard, or perhaps by a sailor with a bagpipe or a fiddle."

14

# ARRIVAL

A doctor who made a journey on a slave ship reported that the slaves sang as well as danced—"but not for their own amusement. The captain ordered them to sing, and they sang songs of sorrow. Their sickness, fear of being beaten, their hunger, and the memory of their country are the usual objects."

In mid-afternoon came the second meal—much like the first—and then the Africans were stowed back into their crowded, airless, foul-smelling quarters. It was a rare voyage that did not lose numbers of slaves to disease, suicide, or sheer despair. Between 1680 and 1688, when the slave trade flourished, the English Royal African Company shipped 60,873 Africans to the New World; 14,387 of them did not survive the frightful passage.

Conditions aboard the slave ships improved somewhat in ensuing decades, but thousands more lost their lives. An unknown number died in rebellion, and there were instances of an entire cargo being dropped overboard when an illegal slaver was chased by British naval vessels. According to an official estimate made in 1789, one out of eight slaves perished on the journey across the Atlantic; many others would never wholly recover from the diseases and injuries suffered on the crossing.

A verse attributed to a pirate slaver tells the grim story:

# BLACK BONDAGE

*We started them upon a voyage with a cargo*
  *full of slaves.*
*It would have been better for those poor souls*
  *to be going to their graves.*
*The plague and fever came on board, swept*
  *half of them away.*
*We dragged their bodies to the rails and threw*
  *them in the sea.*

Many who survived this long ordeal may be for-
given if at times in their future lives they felt that
those who perished along the way were the lucky ones.

TWO

# *WORK*

Africans were brought to this country to work, and work they did—on the cotton plantations of Mississippi and in the tobacco fields of Virginia, in Alabama's rich black belt, in Louisiana's sugar parishes, and in the disease-ridden rice swamps of Georgia and South Carolina. Conditions varied from state to state—Virginia, for example, had a much better reputation than places farther to the south; from plantation to plantation—some small owners were despised by the wealthier ones and even by their own class for the way they treated their bondsmen; and from job to job on a given plantation—house servants, the "black aristocracy," had a far easier time of it than field hands. But for most slaves, given the job of cultivating immense stretches of land and bringing in the great staple crops of the South, the working day was long and hard.

It began before daybreak and lasted until dark, five and sometimes six days a week. In the words of an Alabama man: "Sunup to sundown was for field niggers." Men and women alike were roused at 4 or 5 a.m., generally by the blowing of a horn or the ringing of a bell. "Bells and horns!" a former slave exclaimed many years after the Emancipation. "Bells for this and horns for that! All we knowed was go and come by the bells and horns!" A planter in Alabama added his own little touch to the horn: "To make them get off quickly after their horn is blown, I always whip the last one out."

A visitor to a prosperous and efficiently run plantation in the lower Mississippi valley described a field gang he saw marching to work one morning:

"First came, led by an old driver carrying a whip, forty of the largest and strongest women I ever saw together; they were all in a simple uniform of bluish check stuff; the skirts reaching little below the knee; the legs and feet bare; they carried themselves loftily, each having a hoe over the shoulder, and walking with a free and powerful swing, like *chasseurs* on the march. Behind them came the cavalry, thirty strong, mostly men, but a few of them women, two of whom rode astride on the plow mules. A lean and vigilant white overseer, on a brisk pony, brought up the rear."

# WORK

By the break of day they were already at work, under the eyes and whips of Negro drivers and a white owner or overseer, plowing, hoeing, picking, doing the labors appropriate to the season. On some plantations the workers were permitted to leave the fields in the afternoons, after completing their day's tasks, but in a busy period a man might find himself plowing by moonlight. During the harvest season on sugar plantations, Negroes were worked sixteen to eighteen hours a day, seven days a week—longer hours than convicts were permitted to work in several of the Southern states. A woman who was raised in Louisiana reminisced: "To them what work hour in, hour out, the sugar cane fields sure stretch from one end the earth to the other."

As much might have been said about the tobacco fields or the cotton fields. When cotton was ready for picking, each field hand was given a quota. Although the more adept worker might complete his assignment before sundown and so gain an hour or two of free time or earn a little money by extra picking, a hard-driving overseer could make this difficult. An unusually harsh Florida slaveholder boasted: "I work my niggers in a hurrying time till eleven or twelve o'clock, and have them up by four in the morning."

Here is a slave's description of the routine on a cotton plantation operated by a demanding planter:

"In the latter part of August begins the cotton picking season. At this time each slave is presented with a sack. A strap is fastened to it, which goes over the neck, holding the mouth of the sack breast high, while the bottom reaches nearly to the ground. Each one is also presented with a large basket that will hold about two barrels. This is to put the cotton in when the sack is filled. The baskets are carried to the field and placed at the beginning of the rows.

"When a new hand, one unaccustomed to the business, is sent for the first time into the field, he is whipped up smartly, and made for that day to pick as fast as he can possibly. At night it is weighed, so that his capability in cotton picking is known. He must bring in the same weight each night following. If it falls short, it is considered evidence that he has been laggard, and a greater or less number of lashes is the penalty. . . .

"The day's work over in the field, the baskets are 'toted' or in other words, carried to the gin-house, where the cotton is weighed. No matter how fatigued and weary he may be—no matter how much he longs for sleep and rest—a slave never approaches the gin-house with his basket of cotton but with fear. If it falls short in weight—if he has not performed the full task appointed him, he knows that he must suffer. And if he has exceeded it by ten or twenty pounds, in all probability his master will measure the next day's task accordingly. So whether he has too little or too much, his approach to the gin-house is always with fear and trembling. Most frequently they have too little, and therefore it is they are not anxious to leave the field. After weighing, follow the whippings; and then the baskets are carried to the cotton house, and their contents stored away like hay, all hands being sent in to tramp it down. If the cotton is not dry, instead of taking it to the gin-house at once, it is laid upon platforms, two feet high, and some three times as wide, covered with boards or planks, with narrow walks running between them.

"This done, the labor of the day is not yet ended, by any means. Each one must then attend to his respective chores. One feeds the mules, another the swine— another cuts the wood, and so forth; besides, the packing is all done by candle light. Finally, at a late hour, they reach the quarters, sleepy and overcome with the long day's toil."

By the age of six or seven, children were ready to do odd jobs around the plantation—picking up trash in the yard, raking leaves, tending a garden patch, minding babies, carrying water to the fields. By the age of ten, they were likely to be in the fields themselves, classed as "quarter hands." A woman in Alabama recalled: "Soon as I was ten, Old Master, he say, 'Git this here nigger to the cotton patch.'" She was fortunate. A planter in Alabama sent children into the fields with their mothers at the age of five; he reasoned that it kept them out of trouble.

Another former slave who was brought up on a cotton plantation told how he and his friends would try to escape going into the fields without shoes on fall mornings when there was frost on the ground:

"To keep warm we would wrap up in our sacks and hide under the cotton baskets, but the overseer would find us and kick the baskets from over us and run us out to work in the frost. If you picked one or two hundred pounds one day, you had that amount to pick every day or get punished."

There were few exemptions from labor on a plantation. A new mother was customarily permitted a four-week respite from field work after the birth of her baby, during which time she was given relatively light indoor tasks such as sewing or spinning. But after the four weeks, out she went to the field again, returning several times during the day to nurse her infant, or actually carrying the baby into the field with her.

As a rule, the fifteen-hour day in the fields was broken twice—at 8 a.m. for breakfast and at about noon for a midday meal. The second break might last from fifteen minutes to two hours, depending on the heat of the day ("ninety degrees in the shade" was often an accurate report of the temperature), the condition of the crop, the rules of the plantation, and the disposition of the overseer, who had to account to the plantation owner for any failure to produce a profitable crop.

The most common item in the slave diet was corn, usually ground into meal and cooked in the form of hoecakes (so called because they were originally baked on a hoe). Added to this usually was three or four pounds of salt pork or bacon a week. On more prosperous plantations, there would be a few vegetables in season and other extras. One former slave remembered as a child eating from a long trough in the back yard of the master's house. Bending over and using their hands, the black children scooped into their mouths a mash of vegetables, corn bread, and milk. By and large, the quantity of food in the basic "hog and hominy" menu seems to have been adequate, if, as one observer noted, "coarse, crude and wanting in variety."

It was a great event in a slave's life to find a treat outside his usual diet. Looking back on his first day in his owner's kitchen after being "promoted" from a field hand to a house servant, a Kentucky man remembered discovering some bread in the pantry: "I took piece after piece, and skimming the fat from the top of the boiling pot with them, I made such a meal as I never had in my life before, overjoyed at being placed in a situation where I could satisfy my appetite."

On some plantations, particularly the smaller ones, hunger was a natural state of things. "It was work hard, git beatings and half-fed," recalled a woman who was brought up in Louisiana. "They brung the victuals and water to the fields on a slide pulled by a old mule. Plenty times they was only a half barrel water and it stale and hot, for all us niggers on the hottest days. Mostly we ate pickled pork and coarse bread and peas and beans and 'taters. They never was as much as we needed."

By any standards of the nutritional needs of people who used up so much physical energy over so long a laboring day, this woman was certainly correct. Despite the popular hunting of small animals and the fishing allowed in most places, there were doubtless many slaves who did not receive all that their hard-worked bodies required. As a man who served under a particularly parsimonious master put it: "I can say, from a ten years' residence with Master Epps, that no slave of his is ever likely to suffer from the gout, super-induced by excessive high living."

But probably it was the monotony of the diet—the corn cakes day in, day out—rather than the insufficiency that prompted workers to risk pilfering food from the plantation smokehouse and chicken roost, a widespread practice throughout the South and a cause of continuing dismay and vexation for plantation owners. A quick-witted slave in Alabama, charged with stealing a turkey, explained: "When I tuk de turkey and eat it, it got to be a part of me." Thus, he reasoned, since he was himself the property of his master, just like the turkey, no theft had actually occurred.

The houses to which the workers returned to cook their suppers of corn cakes and take their few hours of rest before the driver's horn roused them to a new day of toil were simple in the extreme. The "nigger yard" was generally made up of two lines of log cabins some distance from the owner's house. A single room about twelve square feet might serve a family. It would probably have a window but was not likely to have a finished floor. Ordinarily, there would be a fireplace of stones, twigs and grasses for heat and for cooking, and a few pieces of furniture—a table, a bench or two, bunks for sleeping. Children often made do with a bundle of rags on the dirt floor.

"The softest couches in the world are not to be found in the log mansions of the slave," wrote Solomon Northup, a free Negro who was kidnapped and sold into slavery. Northup's bed, on a poor plantation, consisted of a plank twelve inches wide by ten feet long, a stick of wood for a pillow, and a coarse blanket for bedding. He noted that moss was available as a blanket, but, unfortunately, it bred fleas. Northup's cabin had no windows, which, he pointed out, was no great loss since the crevices between the cabin's logs let in plenty of light, not to mention rain and cold in winter, and gnats and mosquitos in the summer.

The slave quarters varied greatly from plantation to plantation. On the few showplace plantations of the South they were likely to consist of well-constructed frame houses, with wooden floors, shingle roofs, shuttered windows, and garden plots, but elsewhere they could be quite different. A graphic description of one poor set of quarters was left by Josiah Henson, who grew up on a plantation in Maryland and may have been the model for Uncle Tom in Harriet Beecher Stowe's famous book, *Uncle Tom's Cabin*. Henson wrote:

"We lodged in log huts, and on the bare ground. Wooden floors were an unknown luxury. In a single room were huddled, like cattle, ten or a dozen persons, men, women and children. All ideas of refinement and decency were, of course, out of the question. There were neither bedsteads, nor furniture of any description. Our beds were collections of straw and old rags, thrown down in the corners and boxed in with boards; a single blanket the only covering. . . . The wind whistled and the rain and snow blew in through the cracks, and the damp earth soaked in the moisture till the floor was as miry as a pig-sty. Such were our houses. In these wretched hovels were we penned at night, and fed by day; here were the children born and the sick—neglected."

Two examples of slave quarters in the South

# WORK

A woman who had been a slave in Alabama recalled:

"We had old ragged huts made out of poles and some of the cracks chinked up with mud and moss and some of them wasn't. We didn't have no good beds, just scaffolds nailed up to the wall out of poles and the old ragged bedding thrown on them. That sure was hard sleeping, but even that feel good to our weary bones after them long hard days' work in the field."

Visitors from other countries were taken aback by their first sight of the slave cabins—their earthen floors littered with firewood and shavings; poultry running about; an open ditch for sewage; half-naked children playing among the embers. A British visitor called the quarters "something between a haunt of monkeys and a dwelling place of human beings."

A woman brought up in Kentucky remembered rolling herself up in a quilt on the cabin's dirt floor on cold winter nights and trying to get as close as she could to the fire; more than once she got so close that the quilt was set ablaze.

Keeping warm in the winter was a serious problem for field hands. Blankets were issued in most places every couple of years, but since the climate was relatively mild, the people were rarely given woolly sweaters or thick coats in which they might bundle up on January nights. The youngest children were not troubled with clothing at all; they ran naked. As cooler weather came on, they might be provided with a sack, in which holes had been cut for the head and arms.

The normal plantation practice was to issue clothing twice a year. Men were given a pair of cotton trousers and a shirt in the summer, and a jacket as well as a pair of heavier, woolen trousers and shirt in the winter. The coarse cloth, according to a Virginia man, "was jus' like needles when it was new. Never did have to scratch our back. Jus' wiggle yo' shoulders an' yo' back was scratched." The famed Negro educator Booker T. Washington recalled that as a boy he could imagine no torture, outside of having a tooth pulled, that was equal to putting on a new flax shirt.

Women were given short petticoats and loose gowns made of a rough-textured fabric called homespun. When a generous master provided them with a colorful bolt of cloth out of which they might make a dress or turban for Sunday wear, it was an occasion for rejoicing. Since a slave's entire wardrobe might amount to a single outfit that was subject to extremely hard wear all week, nights and weekends had to be given over to washing and mending; in many places, the ordinary outfit for field work was an assortment of rags.

Among the items that most slaves apparently were not allowed in summer months were shoes—thereby increasing their chances of coming down with hookworm or tetanus—and the shoes they received in colder months were coarsely made and very rough on the feet.

A British visitor traveling through the slave states around 1840 concluded that inmates of the state prisons "were very much better off in food, raiment and accommodations and much less severely worked than those men, whose only crime was that they were of a darker color than the race that held them in bondage."

The combination of hard, sometimes exhausting toil and inferior diet, scanty clothing and unsanitary housing led, predictably, to health problems. A Georgia planter attributed the prevalence of disease in his area to "small, smoking cabins built flat upon the ground, with no windows or aperture for ventilation. . . ." The voodoo bags that many of the slaves wore did not guarantee immunity from such serious diseases as cholera, dysentery, and pneumonia.

Slaveowners had every reason to be concerned over the health of their charges. In the 1850's a prime field hand might cost as much as $1,500, and prices for skilled workers went still higher, so that even the least humane planter wanted the people in his service kept well. A traveler in Virginia, surprised to see a group of Irish workers draining a tobacco field, asked the planter why he had hired white men for the job instead of using his black hands. "It's dangerous work," the planter explained, "and a Negro's life is too valuable to be risked at it. If a Negro dies, it's a considerable loss, you know."

One overseer told a visitor a cautionary tale of a slave who complained that he couldn't work:

"I looked at his tongue and it was right clean, and I thought it was nothing but damned sulkiness. So I paddled him and made him go to work; but two days after, he was underground. He was a good eight-hundred-dollar nigger, and it was a lesson to me about taming possums that I ain't going to forget in a hurry."

The most respected planters and their wives felt a genuine responsibility for their workers, as well as simple human compassion, and lived up to their responsibility by establishing clean, well-run hospitals and nurseries. "Once a nigger gets in there," said an overseer, referring to his plantation's hospital, "he'd like to live there for the rest of his life." Plantation mistresses were celebrated for nursing black children through their illnesses—just as black "mammies" nursed white children. One rice planter set up a house on high ground where youngsters could stay during the summers, while their parents labored in the malaria-ridden fields. (The planter and *his* family were likely to spend the summer at the mountains or seashore.)

But medical science was not at its height in the nineteenth century, and not all masters were either knowing enough or sympathetic enough to care properly for ailing slaves. In some places doctors were called in to treat blacks as well as whites, but as a rule doctors were saved for only the most serious cases. A minister who lived in Georgia for several years wrote of the slaves' medical care: "When sick their physicians are their masters and overseers, in most cases, whose skill consists in bleeding and in administering large portions of Epsom salts, when the whip and cursing will not start them from their cabins." It was an exceptional field hand who lived to a ripe old age. On the sugar plantations of the Gulf Coast, laborers were reportedly worked to death in six to eight years.

Just as there were clean, carefully tended sick rooms on some plantations, so there were the opposite on others. Fanny Kemble, an English actress who lived on her husband's plantation in Georgia for a time, left this description of the lying-in room of its infirmary:

"Here lay some burning with fever, others chilled with cold and aching with rheumatism, upon the hard, cold ground, the draughts and dampness of the atmosphere increasing their sufferings, and dirt, noise and stench and every aggravation of which sickness is capable combined in their conditions. . . ."

Throughout the South, there were slaves whose lots were better than those described here—and, indeed, compared favorably to those of many white workers in

Northern factories. Negroes who served as cooks, servants, and handymen on showcase plantations tended to live in relative comfort. A number actually slept in the main house; on prosperous estates each young white girl was likely to have a young black girl companion and servant who might sleep at the foot of her bed. These domestics enjoyed leftovers from the master's table and could wear the mistress' cast-off clothing.

Pride in the special role of house servant comes through in this recollection of a former valet who served a wealthy Kentucky family named Reed:

"Listen, whilst I tell you what de valet do: He dress nice and stan' roun' 'mongst de white folks. He pay 'tickler 'tention ter what Massa an' Missus say—but mos' specially Massa. He open de do'ah when somebody come an' bow 'em out when dey leave. He tell de front-house servan's what-all ter do, an' go wid Massa ever'whar. Great man, Cunnel Reed. So well known in dat pa'ht o' Kaintucky de state couldn't get 'long widout him. An' me, bein' his valet, was likewise recon-nized wherever I go. 'I'se Alfred, de Cunnel's valet!' I'd tell de folks. Dat got me by widout er pass. . . . Lived noble in Kaintucky in de ole days."

The owners made clear distinctions between domestics and field hands, and there was no question as to which group they favored. As a governess in Mississippi observed:

"The Dandy Slave," a sketch that appeared in a Baltimore newspaper in 1861

# WORK

"The field servant is heavy, loutish and slow; his features scarce elevated above the mule, which is his co-laborer. The domestic servant is more sprightly, better clad, more intelligent and animated, apes polite manners and imitates the polished airs of the well-bred 'white folk.'"

The privileged domestics, some of whom even had servants of their own, tended to look down on the less fortunate field hands—as evidenced by this conversation, overheard on a Mississippi plantation, between a coachman and a footman:

"You know dat nigger they gwine to sell, George?" asked the coachman. "No," replied the footman, "he field nigger. I nebber has no 'quaintance wid dat class."

It was not uncommon for a close relationship to develop between master and house servant, and then the black man would be treated as an individual (although, to be sure, an inferior one) instead of as a piece of property. In return, the Negroes took pride in *their* white family: "I remember all 'bout de Hamptons. Fine folks—quality people! Bes' in de Carolinas. Yes suh! Dat's us."

Years after the Emancipation, numbers of elderly Negroes, some of whom had been field hands on humanely managed plantations, looked back with nostalgia on their days of bondage. "They was good to me and treated me fine," said a Georgia man of his owners. "Oh, yes, they whipped me but only when I needed it." And a North Carolina man, recalling his years as a slave, said: "Cullud people better off den, caise if dey in trouble, Massa gwine he'p 'em out. If dey hungry, he gwine give 'em a whole side o' meat."

Even where the owners were decent men, however, and not given to gratuitous cruelties, things were not easy for black people. Even house servants, privileged class though they were, *did* have to work. A woman from Louisiana recalled her girlhood:

"My mistress would surely work me around the house. I had to rise in the morning at four o'clock and sometimes couldn't retire when night came. I had to clean a six-room house and nurse three kids. When I grew older, cooking and the care of the yards were added to my duties."

Nor were their living conditions invariably so much better than those of other slaves. Fanny Kemble observed: "The young woman who performs the office of lady's maid and the lads who wait upon us at table have neither table to feed at nor chair to sit down upon themselves: The boys sleep at night on the hearth by the kitchen fire, and the women upon a rough board bedstead, strewed with a little tree moss." In some ways, Fanny Kemble suggested, these conditions were all the harder to bear for the house servants because they could not help comparing them with the comparative luxuries of the master's home.

The South's prosperity would have been impossible without slave workers
like those shown in this woodcut

# WORK

As for the ordinary field hand, his life was one of grinding labor and minimal comfort. That was to be expected, for he existed only to bring profit to the plantation. Frederick Douglass drew the contrast between the lot of the slave and that of his master, with impassioned eloquence:

"The slave toils," wrote Douglass, "that another may live in idleness; he eats bolted meal so that another may eat the bread of fine flour; he rests his toil-worn limbs on the cold damp ground, that another may repose on softest pillows; he is clad in coarse and tattered raiment, that another may be arrayed in . . . fine linen; he is sheltered only by the wretched hovel, that another may dwell in a magnificent mansion; and to this condition he is bound down as by an arm of iron."

The black men's past was lost in the brutalities of the African slave trade; his future promised nothing but interminable days in the field and exhausted nights, drab clothing and monotonous meals. Moreover, as we shall see, the tragedies of bondage went deeper than these unchanging, unchangeable circumstances of his life.

Yet, miraculously, the black bondsmen managed to draw some hours of joy from their years of hardship—and with their show of spirit, their imagination, and their ability to play and to laugh, they enriched the entire nation.

# THREE

# *PLAY*

One problem that did not weigh heavily upon a slave was what to do with his free time. Leisure was in short supply for field hands. Their precious Saturday afternoons and Sundays were the only opportunities they had for washing, mending, and the other chores that could not be fitted into the dawn-to-dark work week. Those lucky enough to have vegetable plots could tend them on the weekend, and that was also the time when a man or woman might do some extra task and earn a dollar in spending money for a bit of finery like a calico dress. It is not surprising that groups of Negroes could be found sitting around their hut, "lolling, with half-closed eyes, like so many cats and dogs, against a wall, or upon a bank in the sun, dozing away their short leisure hour," doing absolutely nothing but luxuriating in brief, glorious idleness.

What won the attention of observers, however, was not the understandable displays of weariness but the startling outbursts of exuberance. Even after a day's labors, overseers would often be hard put to get the people settled in their huts. White visitors who came upon grown black men "rolling, tumbling, kicking and wallowing in the dust" tended to attribute such antics to a lack of the refining influences of civilization; it was, commented one, "mere animal existence, passed in physical exertion or enjoyment."

There is no denying that the field hands were subject to little in the way of civilizing influence, but a sympathetic observer might have interpreted the seemingly purposeless rollings and tumblings differently— as the expression of a very human need. Day after day, year after year, the black people trudged to the fields to do the same wearying jobs, prevented in some places even from talking together as they worked. The wonder is not that they would give vent to their repressed spirits when they had the chance but that those spirits remained unbroken in spite of the cursing, the whipping, the unremitting toil.

Writing of his youth, Josiah Henson made the point

that even though he served under a particularly crude and greedy master, slavery was not all misery:

"In those days I had many a merry time, and would have had, had I lived with nothing but moccasins and rattlesnakes in Okefenokee Swamp. Slavery did its best to make me wretched; I feel no particular obligation to it; but nature, or the blessed God of my youth and joy, was mightier than slavery. Along with memories of miry cabins, frosted feet, weary toil under the blazing sun, curses and blows, there flock in others, of jolly Christmas times, dances before old massa's door for the first drink of egg nog, extra meat at holiday times, midnight visits to apple orchards, broiling stray chickens and first-rate tricks to dodge work."

Dancing was the great thing. And the great time for it was Saturday night. Keeping rhythm with fiddle or banjo or sticks on tin pans or anything they could find, the slaves improvised dances that were a source of pleasure and puzzlement to gentlemen and ladies accustomed to the sedate measures of the ballroom. Fanny Kemble was taken aback by "all the contortions, and springs, and flings, and kicks, and capers"; others were impressed by the seeming state of ecstasy that came upon the black people at such times.

In addition to the weekends, there were a few holidays. The gathering in of a bumper harvest, for example, might be the signal for a plantation celebration. Corn-husking and hog-killing time were cues for song:

An artist's rendering of a slave party

# PLAY

*Massa's niggers am slick an' fat,*
  *Oh! Oh! Oh!*
*Shine just like a new beaver hat,*
  *Oh! Oh! Oh!*

*Jones's niggers am lean an' po',*
  *Oh! Oh! Oh!*
*Don't know whether dey get 'nough to eat or no,*
  *Oh! Oh! Oh!*

Many masters permitted their people time off on the Fourth of July so that, with the help of a barbecued hog, sweetmeats, peach cobbler, and apple dumpling, they might celebrate the freedoms that were denied to them. Often, before being allowed to get at the food, they had to listen to speeches extolling a man's right to revolt against tyranny.

Asked to speak at a Fourth of July ceremony in Rochester, New York, in 1852, Frederick Douglass sent forth this ringing condemnation:

"What to the American slave is your Fourth of July? I answer, a day that reveals to him more than all other days of the year, the gross injustice and cruelty to which he is the constant victim. To him your celebration is a sham; your boasted liberty an unholy license; your national greatness, swelling vanity; your sounds of rejoicing are empty and heartless; your denunciation of tyrants, brass-fronted impudence; your shouts of liberty and equality, hollow mockery; your prayers and hymns, your sermons and thanksgivings, with all your religious parade and solemnity, are to him mere bombast, fraud, deception, impiety, and hypocrisy—a thin veil to cover up crimes which would disgrace a nation of savages. There is not a nation of the earth guilty of practices more shocking and bloody than are the people of the United States at this very hour."

The year's main holiday was Christmas, when the plantation's people not only were given gifts of clothing, molasses, and tobacco but were allowed several days for "feasting, frolicking and fiddling." As one put it: "When Christmas comes, de eatin's good, with egg nog in the bowl." It was said to be easier, at Christmas, to count the sober slaves than those who were drunk.

Even the particularly mean master under whom Solomon Northup suffered observed this holiday. During the Christmas season, Northup reported, one planter of the neighborhood would give a party to which several hundred Negroes from nearby plantations were invited. They came on mule, in carts, by foot, all in their best array. The men used the stump of a tallow candle to shine their shoes—if they had shoes. The women tied brightly colored handkerchiefs or red ribbons around their heads; the luckiest of them wore cast-off bonnets. An outdoor table loaded with meat and vegetables awaited them, and they danced, flirted, and sang happy songs like:

# PLAY

*Harper's creek and roarin' ribber,*
*Thar, my dear, we'll live forebber,*
*Den we'll go to de Ingin nation,*
*All I want in dis creation*
*Is pretty little wife and big plantation.*

The only Negroes on a plantation who had limitless leisure were the very youngest; they were permitted to run at will, and it was quite usual throughout the South to find small black and white children playing together. But soon they were separated, as the black boys and girls took on their share of labor and their white playmates were sent off to begin an education of sorts.

"There is a cruel pang that comes to every slave's life, which has been little considered," wrote a native Virginian. "It is customary in nearly all households in the South for the white and black children connected with each to play together. The trial I have referred to comes when the Negroes who have hitherto been on this democratic footing with the young whites are presently deserted by their more fortunate companions, who enter upon school-life and the acquaintance of white boys, and, ceasing to associate with their swarthy comrades any longer, meet them in future with the air of the master. This is the dawn of the first bitter consciousness of being a slave; and nothing can be sadder

49

than to see the poor little things wandering about companionless and comfortless."

Few Southern whites of the time enjoyed more than a rudimentary education; illiteracy was widespread. For Negroes, however, beginning around 1800, schooling was forbidden as a matter of public policy. A Mississippi citizen put the white Southerner's feeling in a straightforward phrase: "Knowledge and slavery are incompatible." A judge in South Carolina expressed the general concern in his state over possible slave uprisings when he said, in 1800, that the sole security of the white men rested upon the ignorance of the black man.

Booker T. Washington, the son of a slave and America's most famous Negro educator, observed that "every plantation in the South was an industrial school," where Negroes could learn to become farmers, blacksmiths, wheelwrights, brick masons, engineers, cooks and so forth. But reading was not on the curriculum of the plantation. Southerners feared, with excellent reason, that the ability to read and write could only increase a slave's dissatisfaction with his lot.

But, not unnaturally, the rules against schooling too produced dissatisfaction: "Do you know who it is that sends you to school?" a valued servant once asked the son of his owner.

"Father," replied the boy.

The servant retorted sharply: "No, he doesn't; it's my labor that sends you to school, but I cannot send *my* children to school."

This situation held true throughout the South. A Louisiana woman who had generally fond memories of her master recalled: "If Marse cotched a paper in you hand he sure whup you. He don't 'low no bright niggers round, he sell 'em quick. He always say, 'Book larning don't raise no good sugar cane.'" Another woman told of the fear of Negroes on her plantation that if they were caught learning to write their fingers would be chopped off.

The brilliant Negro leader Frederick Douglass was first taught his ABC's by his mistress in Baltimore, but no sooner did her husband hear of it than he forbade his wife to continue the instruction. He said, in words that summed up the prevailing anxieties and excuses of the slaveholders:

"If you give a nigger an inch, he will take an ell. A nigger should know nothing but to obey his master— to do as he is told to do. Learning would spoil the best nigger in the world. Now, if you teach that nigger to read, there would be no keeping him. It would forever unfit him to be a slave. He would at once become unmanageable, and of no value to his master. As to himself, it could do him no good, but a great deal of harm. It would make him discontented and unhappy."

That a Negro who could read was likely to be a less

docile creature than one who could not was evident, and the attitude that education was useless for a slave seeped into the whole Southern outlook, black as well as white; it sapped the ambition of boys and girls with a clear capacity for learning. One young man, asked by a compassionate white woman why he had never tried to learn to read, answered: "Missis, what for me learn to read? Me have no prospect." And a bright boy in Alabama resigned himself to the fact that "God did not make niggers to learn books."

But there were determined youths who persisted despite all obstacles. For them the desire to learn was strong, stronger even than their fear of displeasing their all-powerful masters. The luckier ones might actually have an owner who taught them himself, as part of a felt obligation. Some had a kindly mistress. When a boy named Aleck asked Fanny Kemble to teach him to read, she resolved to do it despite the laws against teaching slaves. (In Savannah this offense was punishable by a $30 fine or ten days' imprisonment and thirty-nine lashes.) "Some owners," Fanny Kemble wrote to a friend, "have a fancy for maiming their slaves, some brand them, some pull out their teeth, some shoot them a little here and there. . . . Now they do all this on their plantations, where nobody comes to see, and I'll teach Aleck to read, for nobody is here to see, at least nobody who's seeing I mind; and I'll teach every other creature that wants to learn." (A traveler in

Mississippi in 1852 came upon this odd situation—a group of slaves, all of whom could read, belonging to a planter who was illiterate.)

House servants were in the best position to get hold of a book by one means or another—from a Northern traveler perhaps or simply by slipping it out of the planter's library—and many devoted painstaking hours to trying to make sense of it. A woman from Alabama explained:

"None of us was 'lowed to see a book or try to learn. They say we git smarther than they was if we learn anything, but we slips around and gits hold of Webster's old blue-back speller and we hides it till 'way in the night and then we lights a little pine-torch, and studies that spelling book."

The ingenuity and perseverance that were required in pursuit of literacy come through clearly in the campaign waged by a determined Frederick Douglass after his mistress ceased her instruction:

"The plan which I adopted, and the one by which I was most successful, was that of making friends of all the little white boys whom I met in the street. As many of these as I could, I converted into teachers. With their kindly aid, obtained at different times and in different places, I finally succeeded in learning to read. When I was sent on errands, I always took my book with me, and by doing one part of my errand quickly, I found time to get a lesson before my return. I used also to carry bread with me, enough of which was always in the house, and to which I was always welcome; for I was much better off in this regard than many of the poor white children in our neighborhood. This bread I used to bestow upon the hungry little urchins, who, in return, would give me that more valuable bread of knowledge. . . .

"The idea as to how I might learn to write was suggested to me by being in Durgin and Bailey's shipyard, and frequently seeing the ship carpenters, after hewing, and getting a piece of timber ready for use, write on the timber the name of that part of the ship for which it was intended.

"When a piece of timber was intended for the larboard side, it would be marked thus—'L.' When a piece was for the starboard side forward, it would be marked thus—'S.F.' For larboard aft, it would be marked thus—'L.A.' For starboard aft, it would be marked thus—'S.A.' I soon learned the names of these letters, and for what they were intended when placed upon a piece of timber in the shipyard. I immediately commenced copying them, and in a short time was able to make the four letters named.

"After that, when I met with any boy who I knew could write, I would tell him I could write as well as he. The next word would be, 'I don't believe you. Let me see you try it.' I would then make the letters which I had been so fortunate as to learn, and ask him to beat that. In this way I got a good many lessons in writing, which it is quite possible I should never have gotten in any other way."

The most willing teachers often were the planters' own children. A black boy in Georgia took daily trips to the plantation well, which was located near the local schoolhouse, and induced the white students there to teach him a letter at a time. In this way he learned to read. Later he learned to write from a New Jersey mechanic who had settled in Augusta.

It took a Virginia youth, who had been taught by a friend to read words of three letters, eleven years to work his way up to an ability to read the Bible, after he became convinced that he was meant to be a preacher of the Lord:

"It was my great desire to read easily this book. I thought it was written by the Almighty himself. I loved this book and prayed over it and labored until I could read it. I used to go to church to hear the white preacher. When I heard him read his text I would read mine when I got home. This is the way I learned to read the word of God when I was a slave."

The Southerners' fear of education for their black bondsmen was part of a greater fear of outside ideas of any sort infiltrating the slaves' lives. These included, particularly, unorthodox religious ideas. Churchgoers themselves in the main, the planters would have liked the black man to adopt that part of the white man's religion which stressed meekness and resignation. One Georgia planter bequeathed $200 for the religious instruction of his slaves because he had observed that "it developed a stronger sense to obey, as they feared to offend against the obligations of religion."

The planters did their best to prevent slaves from holding their own religious services with their own black preachers and instead compelled them to listen to Southern white preachers, whose message, with rare exceptions, ran along these lines:

"Serve your master. Don't steal your master's turkey. Don't steal your master's chickens. Don't steal your master's hogs. Don't steal your master's meat. Do whatsomever your master tells you to do." As one member of the audience to such a sermon commented: "Same old thing all the time."

"It's the devil who tells you to try to be free," a Baptist minister in Virginia informed a group of slaves. While ministers in the North were campaigning forcefully against the evils of slavery, Southern preachers, both white and black in the service of planters, were promising the people that if they behaved themselves they might hope eventually to enter "the kitchen of heaven." And the kitchen was a considerable improvement over the future painted by the preacher who, in the recollection of a former slave, advised the people to obey their master and mistress " 'cause what you git from them here in this world am all you ever going to git, 'cause you just like the hogs and the other animals —when you dies you ain't no more, after you been throwed in that hole."

But the black people wanted more than the prospect of a hole in the earth or even heaven's kitchen for eternity; they needed more. A religion designed for the interests of the white plantation owners was of small use to them. How seriously could they take a church in which some of their cruelest taskmasters were respected members? (So cruel was one South Carolina Baptist that all his slaves became Methodists.) How seriously could they take clergymen who themselves owned slaves and even allowed men and women to be sold at church meetings? As a Methodist Episcopalian minister, an abolitionist who worked in Maryland, wrote:

"They [the Negroes] hear ministers denouncing them for stealing the white man's grain; but, as they never hear the white man denounced for holding them in bondage, pocketing their wages, or for selling their wives and children to the brutal traders of the far South, they naturally suspect the Gospel to be a cheat, and believe the preachers and the slaveholders to be in a conspiracy against them."

There were white ministers in the South who worked to better the lot of the laborers, but the black people needed their own preachers—and they produced them, some of them men of extraordinary talents, who went from plantation to plantation at considerable risk to hold secret prayer meetings.

At some of the large plantations there was a "praise-house" where the people were permitted to congregate for praying, preaching, and singing. Elsewhere, seeking to escape supervision, the slaves would go off to the woods for their worship. Women might wet quilts and rags and hang them from branches to keep in the sound as their preacher exhorted them and they prayed: "We prays for the end of tribulation and the end of beatings and for shoes that fit our feet. We prayed that us niggers could have all we wanted to eat and special for fresh meat."

Simple desires—and their vision of heaven was simple too. "This is the end," said a woman in her seventies who had worked hard all her life and never been taught to read or write. "I is waitin' now for judgment day and the time when I won't have to work no more. They tells me there is black angels with black wings and I is prayin' I will be one of them black angels."

The religion that grew out of the private worship was a highly emotional, somewhat superstitious variety of the Baptist and Methodist evangelism that was popular among whites in many parts of the South. A preacher of the time described a typical white Baptist service:

". . . the power of God came down upon the congre-

One of the few joys left to black bondsmen was religion. Church services they attended with whites (above) differed considerably, however, from those they conducted when alone.

gation, some cried for mercy, others shouted for glory, some lay prostrate on the floor, others sat with their cheeks all bathed in tears."

A lively scene, but in the slaves' view, it could not hold a candle to the spirit of *their* services:

> *W'ite folks go to chu'ch*
> *An' he never crack a smile;*
> *An' nigger go to ch'ch,*
> *An' you hear 'im laugh a mile.*

The Negroes adapted the Christian forms to their needs, much as communities of whites had done down the centuries, and the new forms of worship, vibrant, spontaneous, uninhibited, with more than a hint in them of the African past, permitted an emotional breakthrough for a people who were physically enchained. It was here, among themselves, away from their white masters and overseers, that they were able to open their hearts and achieve the most direct expression of their deepest longings. Still today we can feel the power of these longings in the enduring spirituals which embodied them:

> *Oh, freedom; oh, freedom;*
> *Oh, Lord, freedom over me,*
> *And before I'd be a slave,*
> *I'll be buried in my grave,*
> *An' go home to my God and be free.*

# BLACK BONDAGE

*There'll be rejoicin',*
*There'll be rejoicin' over me,*
*And before I'd be a slave,*
*I'll be buried in my grave,*
*An' go home to my God and be free.*

*There'll be shoutin',*
*There'll be shoutin' over me,*
*And before I'd be a slave,*
*I'll be buried in my grave,*
*An' go home to my God and be free.*

*There'll be no groanin',*
*There'll be no groanin' over me,*
*And before I'd be a slave,*
*I'll be buried in my grave,*
*An' go home to my God and be free.*

# FOUR

# *PUNISHMENT*

The religion of the black people was a breath of hope, a portion of joy for existences that were sorely in want of hope and joy. It provided some consolation for the indignities and cruelties to which many a slave was subjected.

How cruel "the peculiar institution" of slavery was to the black bondsmen of the South became a matter of hot debate in the decades leading up to the Civil War. Slaveholders, through their apologists, presented themselves as souls of kindness who treated the Negroes in their charge as children—chastizing them a bit when they misbehaved but thinking always of their best interests. (Unlike normal children, these would never be permitted to grow up.) Northern abolitionists, on the other hand, published tales of horrors committed in the South, of people tortured, mutilated, killed in cold blood. Doubtless there were such horrors—just as, doubtless, there were benevolent owners, like the man who never resorted to a whip because "I cannot punish people with whom I associate every day"; but the average slave's lot in all likelihood resembled neither the unmitigated misery chronicled by the abolitionists nor the rosy picture drawn by Southern politicians and publicists. As one former slave remarked: "The slaveholders are neither more nor less than men, some of whom are good and very many are bad." (Most Southern whites owned no slaves at all, and only a small minority of the slaveholders owned more than twenty.)

Techniques of punishment existed on every plantation, but they varied greatly in degree of severity—depending mainly, it seems, on how prosperous the plantation was (poorer owners were under a compulsion to drive their workers harder) and on the nature of the master and, more especially, of his overseer.

Overseers as a class were widely despised. Solomon Northup, who labored on a struggling Louisiana plantation where "the crack of the lash and the shrieking of the slaves can be heard from dark till bed time . . . any day almost during the entire period of the cotton-picking season," commented that "the requisite qualifications in an overseer are utter heartlessness, brutality and cruelty."

That a Negro should have felt this way is not surprising. (On at least one Georgia plantation after the Civil War, the newly freed people agreed to return to their former condition if only the overseer were discharged.) More surprising, many whites shared their opinion of overseers. "They are the curse of the country," said a paternal plantation owner in Virginia, "the worst men in the community." And a Georgia planter wrote: "To him [the overseer] it is of no consequence that the old hands are worked down or the young ones overstrained; that the breeding women miscarry and the sucklers lose their children; that the mules are broken down, the plantation tools destroyed, the stock neglected and the lands ruined." For such reasons, an overseer rarely lasted very long on any one plantation. A planter in Alabama showed what he thought of the whole trade when, in advertising for a foreman, he listed as a prime requirement that the applicant should have *no* previous experience as an overseer.

Yet, whatever their feelings about overseers, the major planters continued to employ them; they felt they needed a white man to supervise any sizable gang of black workers. There are records of owners reprimanding and dismissing overseers for maltreating slaves, but by and large they continued to rely on these unsavory characters to force a full day's work out of their field hands.

Northern abolitionists issued many broadsides against overseers—generally illiterate men in their twenties, drawn from the South's poor-white class—who inflicted cruel punishments for a whim, but the opponents of slavery understood that the real responsibility lay with the planters, who paid the overseers their salaries and judged them not on the basis of their fitness to supervise human beings but on the size of the crops they produced. As a New York minister observed: "It need hardly be added that overseers are in general ignorant, unprincipled and cruel and in such low repute that they are not permitted to come to the tables of their employers, yet they have the constant control of all the human cattle that belong to the master."

Frederick Douglass made the same point more dramatically:

"One of the first circumstances that opened my eyes to the cruelties and wickedness of slavery and its hardening influences upon my old master, was his refusal to interpose his authority to protect and shield a young woman, a cousin of mine, who had been most cruelly abused and beaten by his overseer in Tuckahoe. This overseer, a Mr. Plummer, was like most of his class, little less than a human brute; and in addition to his general profligacy and repulsive coarseness, he was a miserable drunkard, a man not fit to have the management of a drove of mules. In one of his moments of drunken madness he committed the outrage which brought the young woman in question down to my old master's for protection. The poor girl, on her arrival at our house, presented a most pitiable appearance. She had left in haste and without preparation, and probably without the knowledge of Mr. Plummer. She had traveled twelve miles, bare-footed, bare-necked, and bare-headed. Her neck and shoulders were covered with scars newly made, and not content with marring her neck and shoulders with the cowhide, the cowardly wretch had dealt her a blow on the head with a hickory club, which cut a horrible gash and left her face literally covered with blood. In this condition the poor young woman came down to implore protection at the hands of my old master. I expected to see him boil over with rage at the revolting deed, and to hear him fill the air with curses upon the brutal Plummer; but I was disappointed. He sternly told her in an angry tone, 'She deserved every bit of it, and if she did not go home instantly he would himself take the remaining skin from her neck and back.' Thus the poor girl was compelled to return without redress, and perhaps to receive an additional flogging for daring to appeal to authority higher than that of the overseer.

"I did not at that time understand the philosophy of this treatment of my cousin. I think I now understand it. This treatment was a part of the system, rather than a part of the man. To have encouraged appeals of this kind would have occasioned much loss of time, and leave the overseer powerless to enforce obedience. Nevertheless, when a slave had nerve enough to go straight to his master, with a well-founded complaint against an overseer, though he might be repelled and even have that of which he complained at the time repeated, and though he might be beaten by his master as well as by the overseer, for his temerity, in the end, the policy of complaining was generally vindicated by the relaxed vigor of the overseer's treatment. The latter became more careful and less disposed to use the lash upon such slaves thereafter."

The favored instrument of correction throughout the South, as Douglass's example indicates, was the whip. In the words of an abolitionist who lived in Georgia for several years: "Thirty-nine lashes on the bare back, which tear the skin at almost every stroke, is what the South calls a very moderate punishment." That was an overstatement: on some plantations there was little whipping, and many slaveowners took care to use a type of whip that could deliver a stinging sensation yet did not injure the skin. According to a Mississippi man, the buckskin whip in general use had a much worse crack than bite and could scarcely hurt a child:

# PUNISHMENT

"When it is used by an experienced hand it makes a very loud report and stings or 'burns' the skin smartly but does not bruise it. One hundred stripes well laid on with it would not injure the skin so much as ten moderate stripes with a cowhide."

But many masters and overseers did rely generously on their whips—and not always of the gentler type. "The only way to manage niggers is to keep them down," advised a Charleston planter. "Then you can control them, but not else."

Men, women, and children were whipped for every sort of infraction against the system. They were whipped for not getting out of their huts early enough in the morning or for getting back into them late; for not working fast enough; for leaving the plantation without a pass; for fighting among themselves; for petty thefts. According to one account of plantation life, a nursing mother was whipped if she spent too much time away from the field with her baby. A woman from Alabama recalled being beaten when she was a girl for eating a biscuit, and another said she was sometimes beaten severely without knowing why.

Negroes often whipped other Negroes. "Everybody in the South seemed to want the privilege of whipping somebody else," wrote Frederick Douglass. A common punishment on at least one Mississippi plantation was to have the victim led naked into a ring composed of forty or fifty other slaves. As he ran around the ring, they would be exhorted by the overseer to cut at him with the switches or straps they all held.

Solomon Northup reported that his master, a former overseer with a reputation as a "nigger-breaker," liked to quote Scriptures, in particular Luke, chapter 12, verse 47: "And that servant which knew his lord's will, and prepared not himself, neither did according to his will shall be beaten with many stripes." (Stripes were undesirable, however, when a slave was to be sold, since they indicated that he was not thoroughly subservient and might give trouble to his next owner. Therefore, in some places, such as the Sugar House in Charleston, South Carolina, which served as a kind of slave prison, punishment was inflicted with a wooden paddle instead of a whip. The paddle left no scars. For similar reasons, a keeper of a slave pen in Richmond, Virginia, used an instrument made of a broad strip of cowhide. When a visitor remarked that it looked harmless, he was assured: "It can cause as much torture as any other instrument and even more because we can give as many blows with this strip of hide without its leaving any outward sign; it does not cut into the flesh.")

Northup's master set up an extremely harsh punishment schedule. If a dry leaf was found in the cotton or a branch was broken, the picker would get twenty-five lashes. A slave caught standing idle in the field would get a hundred lashes. It was a hundred and fifty to two hundred lashes for quarreling, and five hundred lashes for runaways. In addition to this kind of organized penalty system, there were other, more impromptu punishments. The reminiscences of slaves are filled with instances of masters and overseers and even mistresses bursting into a passion over some slight or imagined offense and brutally beating a helpless man or woman or child. The strokes of a hickory lash, according to a Georgia man who received three hundred as he was suspended from a tree limb, felt like streams of scalding water running down his back; after a hundred and fifty strokes, "the pain became less acute and piercing, but was succeeded by a dead and painful aching which seemed to extend to my very backbone."

Slave reminiscences also include a few, possibly romanticized instances of fighting back—like this one from a Louisiana woman:

"I was whipped several times in slavery—one morning for being late. When I was about sixteen years old, the overseer attempted to whip me about plowing. I had become tired of being whipped. Old Bumpus (the overseer) hit me with a bull whip—drawing blood. I grabbed it—he changed ends and hit me on the head. I then snatched the whip and struck him on the head. This drew blood, making both of us bleed. After fifteen minutes of hard tusselling, he let me go and never attempted to hit me again."

Frederick Douglass observed that overseers preferred to whip those who allowed themselves to be whipped:

"The slave who had the courage to stand up for himself against the overseer, although he might have many hard stripes at first, became while legally a slave, virtually a free man."

The story is told of the grandfather of Dr. Carter Woodson, an eminent Negro educator, who turned the tables one day and whipped an overseer who had attempted to whip him. His master had him tied up for this, and promised: "When I get through with you, Carter Woodson, you'll be sorry that you ever struck a white man." Woodson, an intelligent fellow who was trained as a mechanic and cabinetmaker, was evidently something of a wit as well. He is supposed to have replied: "You don't have to get through with this for me to feel that way, for I am sorry now, sir."

Negro drivers, who served as foremen under the white overseer's supervision and were rewarded with extra favors and gifts, had the job of punishing their fellow slaves. On one Georgia plantation each driver was permitted to inflict a dozen lashes, the head driver could give thirty-six lashes, and the white overseer was allowed to go up to fifty lashes. A Negro woman remembered, as a girl, seeing her uncle deliver a beating to her mother—"he could not help himself"—and a man recalled his distress and confusion when he first learned that his father's work consisted of beating other black men.

A former slave told of her father, who was a driver over the plow hands and the hoe hands:

"Didn' have no overseer—jus' Paw, ter make 'em work. Paw didn' want ter drive de folks, but Massa whip him an' make him. Paw'd come in when de dark came, an' put de whip on de flo', an' set down in er chair. 'Nobody likes de driver,' he say, an' cry till de tears drap in de fireplace. Maw had ter fix him some hoecake 'fore he feel good ergain."

In some places, however, a kind of black solidarity seems to have developed between drivers and ordinary hands. Solomon Northup reported that during his eight years as a driver, "I learned to handle the whip with marvelous dexterity and precision, throwing the lash within a hair's breadth of the back, the ear, the nose, without, however, touching either of them." The slaves presumably being punished would cooperate by pretending to "squirm and screech as if in agony although not one of them had in fact been even grazed."

The best masters took care to warn their overseers that excessive punishment—say, over twenty lashes—would not be tolerated. A planter in Virginia went on record as stating that correction, when needed, should be applied "with no other weapon than a hickory switch." But in this case, as presumably in others, the overseer paid little heed to the written rule.

73

Some overseers seemed to take peculiar satisfaction in trying out variations on the ordinary whipping process by forcing the victim to assume an especially painful or demeaning position or by using versions of the whip capable of inflicting extra pain. A favorite was the cat-o'-nine-tails, which had nine rawhide thongs to it instead of just one. An Arkansas woman told of a mean overseer: "When he go to whip a nigger, he make him strip to the waist, and he take a cat-o'-nine-tails and bring the blisters, and then bust the blisters with a wide strop of leather fastened to a stick handle. I seen the blood running outen many a back, all the way from the neck to the waist!" There were also memories of overseers dousing blisters with turpentine and bathing raw cuts in brine.

Instead of subduing a victim, such viciousness might have the effect of driving him to run away to the nearby woods or swamp. One tale centers on a slave who struck his owner during an attempted whipping and ran off. He dug a large hole, made a bed of leaves for himself inside, and covered it over with branches. He found a large club with which he killed birds and small game, and now and then he slipped back to the plantation to visit his mother. He is said to have lived this life until freedom came.

In some places wooden stocks were used as supplementary punishment. These consisted of two heavy slabs of timber, with holes into which a man's ankles or hands or head could be locked. Aware of how much the Negroes cherished their brief weekends, some planters imprisoned troublesome workers in cells or stocks while their fellows enjoyed their hours of rest and play. One planter wrote: "So secured in a lonely quiet place, where no communication can be held with anyone, nothing but bread and water allowed, and the confinement extending from Saturday when they drop work, until Sabbath evening will prove . . . effective."

An abolitionist who for a decade lived near Wilmington, South Carolina, told of a captured runaway who was confined to the stocks day and night for a week, with a flogging every morning. The second week he was made to labor in the fields all day with a heavy chain fastened around his neck, and was confined for the night in the stocks. On more than one plantation, potential runaways were forced to work in irons.

The worst atrocities, it is only fair to emphasize, stand out as exceptions to the general conduct of plantations. Those owners and overseers who indulged in them seem as often as not to have been half demented or simply drunk. "If there is anything I like better than my drink," a Texas slaveholder is supposed to have said, "it is whipping a nigger." This 200-pound man had the reputation in the Negro quarters of stamping up and down on a slave's back for amusement.

Such men were despised by the better class of planter, and there were cases of whites being brought to trial for killing or maiming Negroes. But the penalties were small. In Georgia, for example, "unnecessary and excessive whipping, beating, cutting or wounding or by cruelly and unnecessarily biting or tearing with dogs" was considered merely a misdemeanor. A planter in Alabama convicted of killing a slave by beating him over the head with a club, then kicking and whipping him for two hours without let-up, was sentenced to two months' imprisonment and a $500 fine. When a slaveowner in Richmond shot and killed a field hand who was resisting being whipped by his overseer, the local newspaper commented: "Mr. Taylor did what every man who has the management of negroes ought to do; enforce obedience or kill them."

A black man could hardly look for comfort to the laws of the Southern states, which had been written by representatives of slaveholders for the benefit of slaveholders. Under these laws, the slave's time and labor were carefully controlled by his owner. He had no civil or political rights whatever and could own virtually nothing. He was a chattel, an item of personal property, and he could be sold to the highest bidder or willed to heirs or given away as a gift. His family connections were not recognized by law. Even if he managed to gain his freedom, he was subject to numerous restrictions that did not apply to white citizens.

# PUNISHMENT

Declared a justice of the North Carolina Supreme Court: "The power of the master must be absolute to render the submission of the slave perfect." The Georgia Supreme Court ruled that even if an owner should "exceed the bounds of reason in his chastisement, the slave must submit. . . ."

Throughout the South, the evidence of one white man was enough to convict a slave, whereas a black man, even if he was free, was not permitted to testify against a white. The meaning of this arrangement was spelled out by a Northern abolitionist:

"Supposing—to take an extreme case by way of illustration—a planter, or overseer, in the presence of five hundred Negroes, was to arrest a slave, tie him hand and foot, and cut him to pieces, inch by inch, no legal punishment could reach him, and no legal body investigate the crime unless a white man was a witness of the barbarity. The laws refuse to accept Negro evidence in any case, whether it be against or in favor of a white man."

So, except for minimal requirements that they be fed and clothed and not "excessively" abused, slaves were at the mercy of the temperament of their masters and the good natures of their overseers, who, as Frederick Douglass wrote, acted as accuser, judge, jury, and advocate all rolled into one. Those fortunate enough to have a decent owner might escape the worst abuses of slavery; those less fortunate would suffer them. Public opinion offered a degree of protection, but public opinion without the backing of strong laws is an undependable shield.

The vast majority of alleged offenses by Negroes were handled right on the plantation—which, in Douglass's words, was "a little nation within itself, having its own rules, regulations and customs"—but some serious cases found their way into the courts. Since putting a slave in jail meant a loss of money for his owner, imprisonment was relatively rare—though a visitor to a Baltimore penitentiary in 1835 found a man being held there for the crime of *stealing his own wife*—that is, attempting to free her from her servitude. The main punishments meted out by Southern courts for more serious crimes, such as assaults on whites, were whipping and branding. In cases of murder or insurrection, the punishment was hanging—an event that was often attended by large numbers of spectators. The governor of South Carolina conceded in 1855 that the laws regarding Negroes were rarely in accord with justice or humanity, and he found it necessary to set aside lower-court punishments in a majority of cases.

The laws of the South, designed to protect the investment of the planters in their human property, were enforced both by officials, such as sheriffs, and by quasi-official bands, notably the "slave patrols." These patrols, which existed in some form in every Southern state, had the job of keeping watch for Negroes who were away from their plantations without a pass. In many communities, as one reminiscence has it, they performed their jobs "carelessly, indifferently, or not at all." Still, they represented the planters' natural reluctance to have a valuable piece of property run off, as well as the fear of a black conspiracy which troubled whites throughout the South at various times during the eighteenth and nineteenth centuries.

The patrols—known among the slaves as "patty-rolls," "patter-rollers," "patter-roses," and "paddle-rollers"—rode their rounds in sizable bands, on horseback at night. Slaves attending unauthorized meetings sometimes prepared a welcome for the horsemen:

"Old Jim [the preacher] would keep a knot of lightwood handy, an' he'd stick hit close to de fire to draw de pitch out it. When de patrollers come to de door 'twas already hot, you see. Preacher would run to de fireplace, git him a light an' take dat torch an' wave hit back an' fo'th so dat de pitch an' fire would be flyin' ev'y which a way in dese patterollers' faces. Out de doors de slaves would go; dar was a mighty scramble an' scuffle in de dark, an' de slaves would scatter in all directions. You see, patterollers was mostly atter de preacher 'cause he was de leader o' de meetin'. Was a terrible lashin' comin' to him dat got caught. . . ."

Since the leading citizens avoided duty with the patrols, they for the most part were made up of men who owned few if any slaves, were far from successful in life, and seemed to find satisfaction in tormenting persons on a notch lower than themselves in the Southern social structure. They were looked down on by both masters and slaves as "poor white trash." Any Negro they came upon who lacked a pass could expect a beating—so severe at times that owners complained about the damage done to their people.

The patrols inspired fear, but they also inspired humorous tales—like this one from a Virginia man:

"There was ways of beating the patter-rollers. De best way was to head 'em off. I 'member once when we was gonna have a meetin' down in de woods near de river. Well, dey made me de lookout boy, an' when de paddyrollers come down de lane past de church— you see dey was 'spectin' dat de niggers gonna hold a meetin' dat night—well, sir, dey tell me to step out f'm de woods an' let 'em see me. Well, I does, an' de paddyrollers dat was on horseback come a chasin' arter me, jus' a gallopin' down de lane to beat de band. Well I was jus' ahead of 'em, an' when they got almost up wid me I jus' ducked into de woods. Course de paddyrollers couldn't stop so quick an' kep' on 'roun' de ben', an' den dere came a-screamin' an' cryin' dat make you think dat hell done bust loose. Dem old paddyrollers done rid plumb into a great line of grape vines dat de slaves had stretched 'cross de path. An' dese vines tripped up de horses an' throwed de ole

"A ride for Liberty: The Fugitive Slaves." Painted in oil by Eastman Johnson during the 1860's

paddyrollers off in de bushes. An' some done landed mighty hard. . . ."

Like so many of the events in the black people's lives, the patrols also served as the inspiration for songs:

> *Run, nigger, run; de patter-roller catch you;*
> *Run, nigger, run, it's almost day.*
> *Run, nigger, run; de patter-roller catch you;*
> *Run, nigger, run, and try to get far away.*
>
> *De nigger run, he run his best;*
> *Stuck his hand in a hornet's nest,*
> *Jumped de fence and run through de paster;*
> *Marsa run, but nigger run faster.*

The patrols were sometimes accompanied on their rounds by bloodhounds, and it was not unusual for trained dogs to be used to hunt down runaways. There were men who specialized in this trade, who made their living with the help of "nigger dogs." In addition to being useful in tracking runaways, the dogs served to instill fear into the Negroes of a given area and so discourage thoughts of flight. Those who dared to run off anyway had to take account of the dogs—like the young Virginia man who spread wild onions over his track and so threw them off the scent.

Frederick Law Olmstead, a journalist who traveled around the South before the Civil War, came upon a planter in Tennessee who put on an impromptu show of a dog for the edification of some children of his locality. Having called together ten children, seven black and three white, he announced:

"Just look here! Here's a reg'lar nigger dog; have it to ketch niggers when they run away, or don't behave. . . . See what teeth she's got, she'd just snap a nigger's leg off. . . . See how strong its jaws be; he says all he's got to do when a nigger don't behave, is just to say the word, and it'll snap a nigger's head right off, just as easy as you'd take a chicken's head off with an ax."

This gentleman was perhaps overly enthusiastic, but the dogs were well able to inflict pain, and more than one runaway felt their fangs in his leg.

The scars left on the slaves from the teeth of a dog or the fist or lash of a fellow man were painful enough, but there was another kind of scar, not visible to the shrewd traders who examined the black backs for evidence of whippings—a scar that cut much deeper into black lives and to this day has not been entirely healed. Most plantation owners seem not to have been guilty of direct physical brutality toward their workers, but even the kindest of them could not always prevent the break-up of black families which was one of the recurring tragedies of slavery as it was practiced in the the South.

# FIVE

# *THE FAMILY*

Entire African tribes were decimated as their members were uprooted from their homes and transplanted abruptly to the New World by traders who considered them scarcely human; the Africans were robbed of their heritage and their place in a community; they lost vital parts of their identities. Family and tribal bonds were severed, and black people found themselves in an utterly strange land, in thrall to men whose appearance, customs, and tongues were entirely unfamiliar.

With the birth and growth of new generations, the Negroes in bondage in America achieved new identities of a sort, identities in large part imposed on them by the masters of the South. They were called by first names—when they were not simply addressed as "boy." Two men of the same name might be distinguished by some physical trait; a plantation might have a Big Sam and a Little Sam. At least one young mistress in Mississippi found a source of amusement in endowing black babies with names like Alexander the Great, Apollo Belvedere, Nicodemus, Queen Victoria, and Coal Black Rose. When a Negro was permitted a surname, it was likely to be that of his master. This stamp of full possession—being given the "family name" of the man who owned them—perfectly symbolized the view of the Southern slaveowner that his Negroes belonged to him body and soul.

The most intimate parts of a slave's life were subject to the master's control. Female slaves were valued less for their qualities as laborers than for their accomplishments as breeders. "The leading industry of the South," a Georgian observed, "was slave-rearing." In 1832 a prominent Virginian called his state "one grand menagerie, where men are reared for the market, like oxen for the shambles."

Girls were encouraged to have children, for the babies became the master's property at birth and their value in dollars and cents would in time far exceed the expense of raising them. In South Carolina in 1853, a boy weighing fifty pounds could bring $500 to his owner. As one plantation owner wrote:

"No inconsiderable part of a farmer's profits being

in little negroes he succeeds in raising, the breeding women, when lusty, are allowed a great many privileges and required to work pretty much as they please. When they come out of the straw, a nice calico dress is presented each one as a reward and inducement to take care of their children."

Girls began having babies at a very young age and continued to have them as long as they were able. To Fanny Kemble, it seemed that "not a girl under sixteen on the plantation but has children, nor a woman of thirty but has grandchildren."

The planter's interest in increasing the numbers and overall value of his chattels, who could be sold or hired out at a substantial profit, was reason enough to encourage sexual promiscuity among his slaves. A woman might have a half dozen children by a half dozen different fathers.

Quite often slave children were fathered too by the master of the plantation or his sons or his overseer. Planters' wives must have been taken aback to see light-colored lads resembling their husbands running about the Negro quarters. The reminiscences of slaves include numerous instances of a mistress persecuting an attractive black woman who had caught her husband's eye, as well as cases of white men beating girls who refused to submit to them. There are also tales of owners selling off their own mulatto children to traders.

So the soil of slavery was far from conducive to the

institution of marriage among a plantation's workers—and yet, as Frederick Douglass wrote, there were many men and women among the slaves who were true and faithful to each other throughout life. Some owners, prompted by religious scruples or a desire for harmony among their people or by simple human feelings, encouraged marriage.

On many plantations the slaves were permitted to follow their own bent in selecting a mate. One man recalled how he first saw his wife-to-be working in a neighboring field. She was about sixteen:

"I'se mighty smit wid dat gal! Roun' face, white teeth and shiny eyes; arms smooth ez sunlight slippin' back an' fer'ahds over de cotton bushes. I aige up close an' say, frien'ly like, 'What yo' name, gal?'

"She look up an' grin. Now if yo' call er strange gal, an' she git mad an' call de overseer, yo' better duck down de fiel' right quick, caise you gwine get whipped. But she grin, an' dat mean it's all right.

" 'My name Lizzie,' she say. 'What yo' name?'

" 'Me, I'se Jake,' I say. 'Kin I come over some time?'

" 'Rickon so,' she say. An' I done so, very nex' night."

Jake had to get the permission of his owner and of Lizzie's owner before they could marry, but in some places, the master had not only the last word as to who would marry whom, but also the first word. It was not extraordinary for a planter to play the role of marriage broker. This could make for an abrupt engagement:

" 'Dis hyar's Anna,' Massa say, 'an' she's gwine be yo' woman.' " On a plantation in Louisiana, the mistress put a girl of fifteen into a room with a man she had never seen before, with the announcement that he was now her husband.

One former slave recalled:

"Marsa used to sometimes pick our wives fo' us. If he didn't have on his place enough women for the men, he would wait on de side of de road till a big wagon loaded with slaves come by. Den Marsa would stop de ole nigger-trader and buy you a woman. Wasn't no use tryin' to pick one, cause Marsa wasn't gonna pay but so much for her. All he wanted was a healthy one who looked like she could have children, whether she was purty or ugly as sin. Den he would lead you an' de woman over to one of de cabins and stan' you on de porch. He wouldn't go in. No sir. He'd stan' right dere at de do' an' open de Bible to de first thing he come to an' read somepin' real fast out of it. Den he close up de Bible an' finish up wid dis verse:

> Dat you' wife
> Dat you' husban'
> I'se you' marsa
> She you' missus
> You married.

Although on some plantations slave weddings were occasions for elaborate ceremonies followed by feasting and celebrating, they might also be rather impromptu affairs. One common ritual, the "broomstick marriage," consisted of placing a broom on the ground and having the couple, who might barely have laid eyes on one another before this moment, join hands and jump over it, whereupon the master would pronounce them man and wife, sometimes adding a short reading from the Bible. "When we step 'cross de broomstick, we was married," one man recalled. "Was bad luck to tech de broomstick. Fo'ks always stepped high 'cause dey didn't want no spell cast on 'em. . . ."

The ordinary slave family was subject to pressures that continually threatened its survival—and not infrequently destroyed it. Kenneth Stampp, whose book *The Peculiar Institution* is an illuminating recent study of slavery in the pre-Civil War South, sums up these pressures:

"In the life of the slave, the family had nothing like the social significance that it had in the life of the white man. The slave woman was first a full-time worker for her owner, and only incidentally a wife, mother, and home-maker. She spent a small fraction of her time in the house; she often did no cooking or clothes making; and she was not usually nurse to her husband or children during illness. Parents frequently had little to do with the raising of their children; and children soon learned that their parents were neither

A nineteenth-century woodcut depicts a wedding ceremony

the fount of wisdom nor the seat of authority. . . . Parents and children might spend some spare hours together in their garden plots, but, unlike rural whites, slaves labored most of the time for their masters in groups that had no relationship to the family. The husband was not the director of an agricultural enterprise; he was not the head of the family, the holder of property, the provider or the protector."

Since a father had little authority over his family and less responsibility, it was not unusual for him to feel small attachment to his offspring. And for women who were forced to spend most of their waking lives in the fields, as Fanny Kemble wrote, motherhood became "mere breeding, bearing, suckling, and there an end."

It was not uncommon for husband and wife to live at different plantations and see each other only two or three nights a week. Many children grew up neglected by their hard-toiling mothers and with barely a memory of their fathers. When planters spoke of a slave "family," they customarily meant only the mother and her children. Where children remembered their father, it might be in a particularly cruel scene—such as seeing him standing helplessly by while his wife was whipped.

The strength of the family was severely undermined as children recognized at an early age that their parents were not in fact in control of their own lives.

Frederick Douglass tells a moving story, doubtless repeated many times in many places in the South, of a woman who was beaten by an overseer as her three small children pelted him with stones and cried, "Let my mammy go! Let my mammy go!" The lesson of his helplessness was learned and relearned by a slave throughout his life. A Memphis house servant named Louis Hughes described in his autobiography his frustration when he heard his wife being beaten in the next room: "I was trembling from head to foot, for I was powerless to do anything for her."

Law as well as custom worked against the growth of strong family ties among Negroes. "The relation between slaves," ruled the North Carolina Supreme Court, "is essentially different from that of man and wife joined in lawful wedlock." The court went on to point out that a marriage between slaves might be "dissolved at the pleasure of either party, or by the sale of one or both, depending upon the caprice or necessity of the owner."

Despite such legalisms and all of the other obstacles, love did grow between black men and women, between parents and their children, and the fear of forced separation was much on their minds. A field hand named Jerry expressed that concern at his marriage to a house servant named Fanny when he made this toast: "Me hope Fanny and myself nebber will be parted from each other or our children." Jerry's wish came true, but many slaves were not so fortunate. There is no more pitiful chapter in the history of slavery than that which recounts the forced break-up of black families.

There were owners who were sensitive to the sufferings caused by such break-ups—like the woman in Virginia who freed her slaves in her will rather than subject them to possible sale by her heirs, because "I cannot satisfy my conscience to have my Negro slaves separated from each other and from their husbands and wives." Others took pains to sell their slaves only in family groups, and only to buyers in the same part of the country, who pledged to keep them together. Moreover, there were numerous instances of planters purchasing a worker's wife or husband from another plantation so that man and wife might be together.

But the kindest masters could not always control the fates of their people. This is strikingly shown in what happened at the plantation of Pimlico in South Carolina, which was celebrated for the good relations existing there between slaves and master—the comfortable cabins, happy children, and generally bright spirits. "On this plantation," one traveler wrote, "I have no doubt, from what I saw, that the slaves are kindly treated and that the patriarchal relation in all its best aspects exists between the master and his poor dependents."

Less than a year after this traveler had paid his visit to Pimlico and been so impressed, the owner of the plantation, General James Gadsden, died. He was heavily in debt, and his slaves were sold to traders and dispersed around the South. It is not unnatural, in view of such disasters, that one of the sorrowful songs of slavery went this way:

> *Dis time tomorrer night*
> *Where will I be?*
> *I'll be gone, gone, gone*
> *Down to Tennessee.*

Not all masters, unfortunately, were possessed of delicate consciences with regard to their workers, and the workers suffered for it. A Northern editor traveling through North Carolina came upon a man whose wife had been sold off after twenty-four years of marriage, their twelve children going with her. He remarried, only to have his second wife sold off after three years.

It was not unheard of for black children to be assigned to different heirs of their owner even before birth; a rich Kentucky man adopted the custom of presenting a small slave to each of his grandchildren. And it was only too common, as exemplified by the Pimlico case, for the members of a black family to be dispersed after their owner's death or as payment for his debts while he still lived.

# THE FAMILY

Advertisements such as the following, which referred to a thirty-five-year-old mother and her fourteen-year-old daughter and eight-year-old son, could be found in newspapers throughout the South: "As valuable a family . . . as ever was offered for sale. . . . The whole will be sold together, or a part of them, as may suit the purchaser." A man who had been separated from his family owing to such a sale put his feelings simply: "Slavery sunders everything we love in dis life, God knows."

A Northern abolitionist traveling about the South came upon a particularly moving scene of forced parting. A young master, owner of a slave family that included two old grandparents, their six children and eighteen grandchildren, had lost heavily at billiards to a New Orleans gambler. The losses included six of his Negroes. As they were being herded into the "nigger car" at the railroad station, the wife of one of the men who had been sold ran after him in tears to give him a small parting gift. As the train pulled out, she threw the package after it, but her gift fell short onto the tracks. Southerners watching the scene seemed highly amused.

The reminiscences of former slaves are filled with anguished scenes of parting. A Virginia man, whose wife and three children were sold off suddenly, stood by the side of the road waiting for them to pass on the first leg of their journey to the Carolinas:

97

"Soon the gang approached in which my wife was chained. . . . She passed and came near to where I stood. I seized hold of her hand intending to bid her farewell; but words failed me; the gift of utterance had fled, and I remained speechless. I followed her for a distance, with her hand gripped in mine, as if to save her from her fate, but I could not speak, and I was obliged to turn away in silence."

This man, Henry "Box" Brown, claimed to have escaped from his owner soon after this, through the ruse of having himself mailed to Philadelphia in a box three feet long and two feet wide. He emphasized that what caused him to escape was the separation from his family, and no other cruelty:

"From the time I first breathed the air of human existence, until the hour of my escape, I did not receive but one whipping. I never suffered from lack of food, or on account of too extreme labor; nor for want of sufficient clothing to cover my person." He wrote that he always thought of his master as a kind man, and added, "Heaven save me from kind masters. . . ."

Josiah Henson, who was only five or six years old when his kindly Maryland master died, gave this description of his family's break-up:

"My brothers and sisters were bid off first, and one by one, while my mother, paralyzed by grief, held me by the hand. Her turn came, and she was bought by Isaac Riley of Montgomery County. Then I was of-

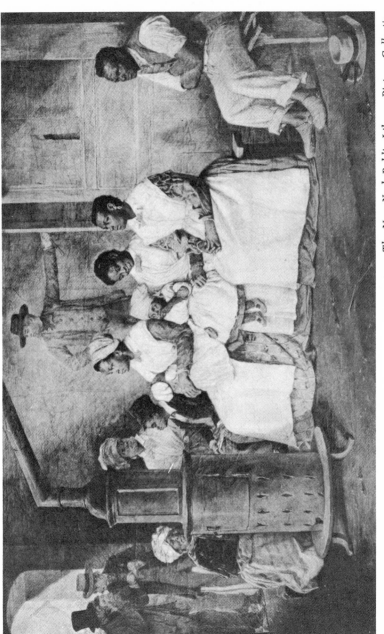

A slave market in Richmond, Virginia

fered to the assembled purchasers. My mother, half distracted with the thought of parting forever from all her children, pushed through the crowd while the bidding for me was going on, to the spot where Riley was standing. She fell at his feet, and clung to his knees, entreating him in tones that a mother only could command, to buy her *baby* as well as herself, and spare to her one, at least, of her little ones. Will it, can it be believed that this man, thus appealed to, was capable not merely of turning a deaf ear to her supplication, but of disengaging himself from her with such violent blows and kicks, as to reduce her to the necessity of creeping out of his reach, and mingling the groan of bodily suffering with the sob of a breaking heart?"

By a happy stroke, the boy Josiah was reunited with his mother, but many children were not. The best they could hope for was that some black family on the new plantation would informally adopt them. It is no wonder that they were able to put a world of private emotion into the hymn that began: "I wonder where my mudder gone / Sing, O graveyard!"

The terror and misery of the slave auction remained with Josiah Henson throughout his life. He wrote:

"The first sad announcement that the sale was to be; the knowledge that all ties of the past are to be sundered; the frantic terror of being sent 'down south'; the almost certainty that one member of a family will be torn from another; the anxious scanning of purchasers' faces; the agony at parting, often forever, with husband, wife, child—these must be seen and felt to be fully understood. Young as I was then, the iron entered my soul."

The slave traders, whom one visitor to the South described as "a compound of everything vulgar and revolting," had little time to spare for the feelings of their human commodities, who were often sold at public auction along with horses, cattle, hogs, and all manner of merchandise. The auctioneers put on a jolly face, like the man in New Orleans who gaily sold a young mother and her two-year-old son:

"Amanda Mix, step forward a little and let the gentlemen see how firm you stand on your corn stalks. There is a beautiful picture. You need not blush, Amanda, you deserve the compliment. Why, gentlemen, there has not been so splendid a lot in this market within my recollection. . . . I say, here is a woman of most excellent parts—young, well proportioned, and strong; as tractable as a lamb, extremely honest and industrious, with a child that in a very few years, will be a mine of wealth to its proprietor; and yet for these inestimable articles the paltry sum of five hundred fifty dollars only has been offered." By such cajolery, the price for mother and child was brought up to seven hundred dollars.

# THE FAMILY

Behind the auctioneer's jollity, of course, lay a simple desire for profit. A man who watched an auctioneer at work in Huntsville, Alabama, wrote in outrage: "In order to force them to bring as much money as possible, the cold-blooded villain deliberately sold man and wife, parents and children, in separate lots." Many slaves had to undergo the indignities of auction more than once. Mary Simpkins, a South Carolina girl who was only twenty-five years old when freedom came, had already been sold and bought three times; at the very first sale, she was separated from her mother.

Traders did their best to keep up the slaves' spirits and appearance (and price) by dressing them in bright new clothes and giving them small treats—some whiskey or tobacco for the men, gaily figured bandannas for the women, toys for the children—to a point where a slave might actually aid in the sale process by speaking highly of himself, if he liked the looks of a potential purchaser: "Buy me, master, I am a good field hand and can work at anything."

Some slaves took open pride in bringing a high price —"I'z a seben-teen hun-dud dol-lah niggah, I iz!"— particularly as it might mean a gift for them from the trader. One former slave explained: "Ef yo' talked up bright an' smaht an' was sol', p'r'aps de niggah-tradah'd give yo' a dollar."

Northerners who visited an auction for the first time were struck by the brutal indignity of the proceedings, as the Negroes, prodded onto a platform in some filthy warehouse, were examined by potential buyers. A historian described one such spectacle:

"Hands were opened and shut and looked at inside and out. Arms and legs were felt as a means of deciding whether they were muscular and regular. Backs and buttocks were scrutinized for the welts that heavy blows with a whip usually left. Necks were rubbed or pinched to detect any soreness or lumps. Jaws were grasped, fingers were run into Negroes' mouths, which were widely opened and peered into. Lips were pressed back so that all the teeth and gums could be seen. This performance closely resembled that of an expert reading a horse's age."

An informative and very moving account of an auction, as seen by one of the slaves up for sale, was set down by Solomon Northup:

"In the first place we were required to wash thoroughly, and those with beards to shave. We were then furnished with a new suit each, cheap, but clean. The men had hat, coat, shirt, pants and shoes; the women frocks of calico, and handkerchiefs to bind about their heads. We were now conducted into a large room in the front part of the building to which the yard was attached, in order to be properly trained, before the admission of the customers. The men were arranged on one side of the room, the women on the other. The tallest was placed at the head of the row, then the next tallest, and so on in the order of their respective heights. Emily was at the foot of the line of women. Freeman [the slave trader] charged us to remember our places; exhorted us to appear smart and lively—sometimes threatening, and again, holding out various inducements. During the day he exercised us in the art of 'looking smart,' and of moving to our places with exact precision.

"After being fed, in the afternoon, we were again paraded and made to dance. Bob, a colored boy, who had some time belonged to Freeman, played on the violin. Standing near him, I made bold to inquire if he could play the 'Virginia Reel.' He answered he could not, and asked me if I could play. Replying in the affirmative, he handed me the violin. I struck up a tune, and finished it. Freeman ordered me to continue playing, and seemed well pleased, telling Bob that I far excelled him—a remark that seemed to grieve my musical companion very much.

"Next day many customers called to examine Freeman's 'new lot.' The latter gentleman was very loquacious, dwelling at much length upon our several good points and qualities. He would make us hold up our heads, walk briskly back and forth, while customers would feel of our hands and arms and bodies, turn us about, ask us what we could do, make us open our mouths and show our teeth, precisely as a jockey examines a horse which he is about to barter for or purchase. Sometimes a man or woman was taken back to the small house in the yard, stripped, and inspected more minutely. Scars upon a slave's back were considered evidence of a rebellious or unruly spirit, and hurt his sale. . . .

"David and Caroline were purchased together by a Natchez planter. They left us, grinning broadly, and in a most happy state of mind, caused by the fact of their not being separated. Seth was sold to a planter of Baton Rouge, her eyes flashing with anger as she was led away.

"The same man also purchased Randall. The little fellow was made to jump, and run across the floor, and perform many other feats, exhibiting his activity and condition. All the time the trade was going on, Eliza [Randall's mother] was crying aloud, and wringing her hands. She besought the man not to buy him, unless he also bought herself and Emily. She promised, in that case, to be the most faithful slave that ever lived. The man answered that he could not afford it, and then Eliza burst into a paroxysm of grief, weeping plaintively. Freeman turned round to her, savagely, with his whip in his uplifted hand, ordering her to stop her noise, or he would flog her. He would not have such work—such snivelling; and unless she ceased that minute, he would take her to the yard and give her a hundred lashes. Yes, he would take the nonsense out of her pretty quick—if he didn't might he be d———d.

Eliza shrunk before him, and tried to wipe away her tears, but it was all in vain. She wanted to be with her children, she said, the little time she had to live.

"All the frowns and threats of Freeman could not wholly silence the afflicted mother. She kept on begging and beseeching them, most piteously, not to separate the three. Over and over again she told them how she loved her boy. A great many times she repeated her former promises—how very faithful and obedient she would be; how hard she would labor day and night, to the last moment of her life; if he would only buy them all together. But it was of no avail; the man could not afford it. The bargain was agreed upon, and Randall must go alone. Then Eliza ran to him; embraced him passionately; kissed him again and again; told him to remember her—all the while her tears falling in the boy's face like rain.

"Freeman damned her, calling her a blubbering, bawling wench, and ordered her to go to her place, and behave herself, and be somebody. He swore he wouldn't stand such stuff but a little longer. He would soon give her something to cry about, if she was not mighty careful, and that she might depend upon.

"The planter from Baton Rouge, with his new purchase, was ready to depart.

" 'Don't cry, mama. I will be a good boy. Don't cry,' said Randall, looking back, as they passed out of the door."

The dreaded journey south, to Alabama or Mississippi or "old debble Lousy-Anna," a fate which slaves were known to mutilate themselves to avoid, was generally made overland on foot. On these "coffles," led by men who were known among the Negroes as "soul drivers," fifty or seventy-five people or more were tied or chained together, marching all day and resting in fields or barns at night. An observer told of seeing ten boys between the ages of six and twelve tied together in pairs by the wrists and all fastened to a rope, shuffling along a dusty road on their way to a slave market. On route, their refreshment was taken at horse troughs and they bedded down in sheds or in the open field.

One former slave left a record of his feelings during the nearly five weeks that he spent in chains as one of a coffle walking from Maryland to South Carolina. One night they stopped at a cheap tavern:

"Our master ordered a pot of mush to be made for our supper; after dispatching which we all lay down on the naked floor to sleep in our handcuffs and chains. The women, my fellow slaves, lay on one side of the room; and the men who were chained with me occupied the other. I slept but little this night, which I passed in thinking of my wife and little children, whom I could not hope ever to see again. I also thought of my grandfather, and of the long nights I had passed with him, listening to his narratives of the scenes through which he had passed in Africa. I at length fell

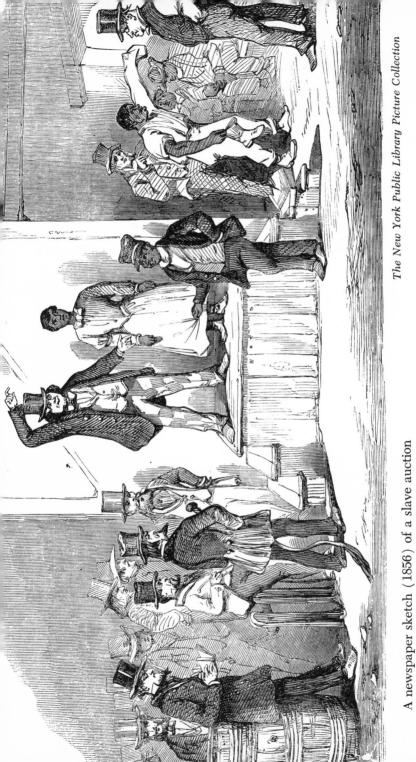

A newspaper sketch (1856) of a slave auction

asleep, but was distressed by painful dreams. My wife and children appeared to be weeping and lamenting my calamity; and beseeching and imploring my master on their knees, not to carry me away from them. My little boy came and begged me not to go and leave him, and endeavored, as I thought, with his little hands to break the fetters that bound me. I awoke in agony and cursed my existence."

On such a journey, which might mean walking twenty-five miles a day for seven or eight weeks in sun and rain, an infant was a distinct nuisance to the slave trader and might abruptly be taken from his mother's arms and given to some casual bystander. Such an incident occurred in Kansas, where a slave trader, puzzled over what to do with a baby ("We can't take it in the wagons and have it squalling all the way"), snatched the child from its mother and presented it to a slaveowner who happened to be on the spot. A witness wrote that "the child was carried off amid the heart-rending shrieks and pleadings of the agonized mother." When Northern visitors questioned slaveowners about such scenes, the plantation men sometimes explained: "These Negroes do not feel these things as we do. They are an altogether inferior race of beings and have no strong affections."

It was in the trader's interest not to drive his coffle too hard on the journey south; he wanted the workers to arrive in fit condition to bring a good price. But the journey was at best arduous—people who died on the way were buried in hastily dug holes. The destination was terrifying—to be "sold south" was a fearsome threat to Negroes in Maryland and Virginia. And the prospect of being separated from family and friends could be unbearable. It was a frequent cause of flight. Thus, by running off, did the slaves demonstrate their "strong affections." Advertisements for runaways frequently contained comments such as: "I think it quite probable that this fellow has succeeded in getting to his wife, who was carried away last spring out of my neighborhood."

Running away was a major form of resistance to the abuses suffered by the South's human chattels. No book about slavery is complete without a chapter on the black man's resistance.

# SIX

# RESISTANCE

It was an article of faith among Southern publicists that black people rejoiced in their servitude. That Southerners should say so and even believe so was to be expected. But more objective observers, too, found that in many places, notably on the most beneficently run plantations and among the best-treated slaves, there did seem to be an air of contentment and mutual affection between blacks and whites. It is striking that during the Civil War, when plantations throughout the South were left in the charge of women and old men, not a single plantation appears to have been taken over by a spontaneous uprising of its black workers. Yet surely Booker T. Washington's mother could not have been the only slave to kneel and pray that "Lincoln and his armies might be successful and that one day she and her children might be free." And there were Negroes who ran off to join the Union Army.

After the Emancipation, a substantial number of Negroes elected to remain with their former masters. As one recalled: "De Major call all his cullud people up to de house. Say to 'em: 'Servan's, you all jus' as free now as yo' Massa!' He stan' thar, straight as when he's wearin' his uniform, an' de tears start down his face. Reckon we gwine leave him? Naw suh!" This kind of reaction may be attributed as much to fear of the strange new freedom the people were being offered as to affection for servitude; whatever the reasons, many years later some former slaves questioned as part of a study were actually nostalgic for pre-war plantation life and unreconciled to the problems that freedom brought.

But the childlike contentment and gaiety of the Negro which impressed some visitors to the South—to them it seemed that he was invariably singing, dancing, and playing games—was only part of the story of the adaptation to bondage, and a superficial part. As a former Virginia slave remarked, in reference to the apparently contented household domestics: "Their broadcloth and calico look fine, but you may examine their persons and find many a lash upon their flesh." When a visitor came to his plantation, he recalled, the people were made to put on their best clothes and were sometimes given rum to liven them up. Then, when the visitor asked whether they loved their master, they would reply that they wouldn't leave him for the world. "The slaves do not speak for themselves," wrote this man in a book issued by Northern abolitionists. "The slave-holding master and his rum are working in their heads, speaking for slavery."

Even where rum was not supplied, a natural suspicion of intrusive white men was enough to account for the common reply to travelers who asked workers whether they wanted to be free. "No, massa," ran the refrain, "me no want to be free, have good massa, take care of me when I sick, never 'buse nigger; no, me no want to be free."

How well advised the slaves were to give such rote answers was dramatized by an incident recounted by Frederick Douglass:

"The real feelings and opinions of the slaves were not much known or respected by their masters. The distance between the two was too great to admit of such knowledge; and in this respect Col. Lloyd was no exception to the rule. His slaves were so numerous he did not know them when he saw them. Nor, indeed, did all his slaves know him. It is reported of him, that riding along the road one day he met a colored man, and addressed him in what was the usual way of speaking to colored people on the public highways of

115

the South: 'Well, boy, who do you belong to?' 'To Col. Lloyd,' replied the slave. 'Well does the Colonel treat you well?' 'No, sir,' was the ready reply. 'What, does he work you hard?' 'Yes sir.' 'Well don't he give you enough to eat?' 'Yes, sir, he gives me enough to eat, such as it is.' The Colonel rode on; the slave also went on about his business, not dreaming that he had been conversing with his master. He thought and said nothing of the matter, until two or three weeks afterwards, he was informed by his overseer that for having found fault with his master, he was now to be sold to a Georgia trader. He was immediately chained and handcuffed; and thus without a moment's warning, he was snatched away, and forever sundered from his family and friends by a hand as unrelenting as that of death. This was the penalty of telling the simple truth, in answer to a series of plain questions. It was partly in consequence of such facts, that slaves, when inquired of as to their condition and the character of their masters, would almost invariably say that they were contented and their masters kind. Slaveholders are known to have sent spies among their slaves to ascertain if possible their views and feelings in regard to their condition; hence the maxim established among them, that 'a still tongue makes a wise head.' They would suppress the truth rather than take the consequences of telling it, and in so doing they prove themselves a part of the human family. I was frequently asked if I had a kind master, and I do not remember ever to have given a negative reply. I did not consider myself as uttering that which was strictly untrue, for I always measured the kindness of my master by the standard of kindness set up by the slaveholders around us."

It was agreeable to most Southern planters to accept their slaves' protestations of loyalty at face value, but Fanny Kemble had a very different reaction. She was escorted everywhere by the bright young son of the plantation's head driver, and one day she suddenly asked him whether he would like to be free. Here is Fanny Kemble's description of his response:

"A gleam of light absolutely shot over his entire countenance, like the vivid and instantaneous lightning; he stammered, hesitated, became excessively confused and at length replied, 'Free, Missis! What for me wish to be free? Oh no, missis, me no wish to be free. . . .' The fear of offending by uttering that forbidden wish—the dread of admitting, by its expression, the slightest discontent with his present situation—the desire to conciliate my favor, even at the expense of strangling the intense natural longing that absolutely glowed in his every feature—it was a sad spectacle, and I repented my question."

A perceptive traveler in Alabama found little honest gaiety in the slave quarters. He wrote of the slaves: "They neither hope nor grumble nor threaten." Making his journey in the 1850's, he found the black man's attitude toward the white man "either sullen, jocose or fawning"; it was rarely frank, and this lack of frankness made it difficult for outsiders to measure what the slaves really felt.

The slaveholders, who took pride in how thoroughly they understood the "character" of the Negro, were at least in some cases taken in themselves by the various poses which their "servants" (respectable masters and mistresses never used the word "slave") adopted as a form of self-defense against a system that left them powerless. Writing in 1837, a shrewd Virginia planter warned that "if his [the servant's] master treats him as a fool, he will be sure to act the fool's part. This is a very convenient trait, as it frequently serves as an apology for awkwardness and neglect of duty."

Now and then, however, a thoughtful Negro would speak honestly in the presence of a white man, and the results could be enlightening, and moving. An elderly gravedigger in Mississippi, for example, once asked a friendly white traveler: "Can you 'splain how it happened in the fust place, that the white folks got the start of the black folks, so as to make dem de slaves and do all de work?"

Before the white man could reply, a young companion of the gravedigger broke in: "Uncle Pete, it's no use talkin'. It's fo'ordained. The Bible tells you that. The Lord fo'ordained the nigger to work and the white man to boss."

Uncle Pete reflected, "Dat's so. Dat's so." Then, in an outburst of despair and defiance, he cried, "But if dat's so, then God's no fair man."

Although nobody ever took a poll of black people to ascertain whether they enjoyed being bondsmen, there is no want of evidence that relations between slaves and masters were less perfect than the slaveholders proclaimed. For example, thievery was a routine fact of plantation life. The ex-slave Josiah Henson offered one explanation for this: "The natural tendency of slavery is to convert the master into a tyrant, and the slave into the cringing, treacherous, false and thieving victim of slavery." Kenneth Stampp, the historian, concluded from a study of the papers of plantation owners that "slaves would take anything that was not under lock and key. Field hands killed hogs and robbed the corn crib. House servants helped themselves to wines, whiskey, jewelry, trinkets and whatever else was lying about."

On some plantations, stealing food was simply a way of supplementing a poor diet, but a good deal of illicit trading went on in many parts of the South, which enabled slaves to dispose of what they had pilfered for a bit of change or some whiskey. Traders would moor their boats at night along the banks of the

Mississippi River and float off before daybreak with their stolen merchandise.

Stealing from fellow slaves appears to have been rare, but any white family was fair game. As a young domestic explained after being chided by her mistress for taking some trinkets: "Law, ma'm, don't say I's wicked; ole Aunt Ann says it allers right for us poor colored people to 'popiate whatever of de wite folk's blessings de Lord puts in our way."

An escapee recalled that he never knew a slave who believed he was doing anything wrong by stealing from his owner:

"The slave sees his master residing in a spacious mansion, riding in a fine carriage, and dressed in costly clothes, and attributes the possession of all these enjoyments to his own labor; whilst he who is the cause of so much gratification and pleasure to another, is himself deprived of even the necessary accommodations of human life."

A young man who ran off from his plantation in Kentucky to join the Union Army during the Civil War reflected:

"Twenty-one years of my life had been spent in one place, working for one family, and all I had to show for that labor was an old pair of trousers, a hickory shirt, a pair of shoes with no socks, and an old hat, none of which were any the better for wear." ( In time this man, Robert Anderson, became a well-to-do farmer in Nebraska.)

Given their circumstances, high-spirited youths like Josiah Henson found that stealing afforded one of the few possible outlets for their impulses toward gallantry:

"At fifteen years of age there were few who could compete with me in work or sport. I was as lively as a young buck, and running over with animal spirits. I could run faster, wrestle better, and jump higher than anybody about me, and at an evening shakedown in our own or a neighbor's kitchen, my feet became absolutely invisible from the rate at which they moved. All this caused my master and my fellow slaves to look upon me as a wonderfully smart fellow, and prophesy the great things I should do when I became a man. My vanity became vastly inflamed, and I fully coincided in their opinions. Julius Caesar never aspired and plotted for the imperial crown more ambitiously than did I to out-hoe, out-reap, out-husk, out-dance, out-everything every competitor; and from all I can learn he never enjoyed his triumph half as much. One word of commendation from the petty despot who ruled over us would set me up for a month. . . .

"Besides these pleasant memories I have others of a deeper and richer kind. I early learned to employ my spirit of adventure for the benefit of my fellow-suffer-ers. The condition of the male slave is bad enough; but that of the female, compelled to perform unfit labor, sick, suffering, and bearing the peculiar burdens of her own sex unpitied and unaided, as well as the toils which belong to the other, is one that must arose the spirit of sympathy in every heart not dead to all feeling. The miseries which I saw many of the women suffer often oppressed me with a load of sorrow. No *white* knight, rescuing fair ones from cruel oppression, ever felt the throbbing of a chivalrous heart more intensely than I, a *black* knight, did, in running down a chicken in an out-of-the-way place to hide till dark, and then carry to some poor overworked black fair one, to whom it was at once food, luxury, and medicine."

From the prevalence of thieving, as well as from widespread arson, the misuse and breaking of tools, the destruction of other property, the carelessness that resulted in injury to farm animals and damage to crops, observers could deduce that slaves and masters did not everywhere constitute one big happy family. But the most common complaint among planters was simply that their workers refused to work very hard. Planters tended to ascribe this reluctance to an innate laziness in the Negro character, but given the conditions of slavery—the long hours, the negligible rewards, the blank future—it is not difficult to understand why a field hand should not have been inclined to exert himself for his master's benefit. As Frederick Douglass explained:

"We knew that if, by extraordinary exertion, a large quantity of work was done in one day, the fact, becoming known to the master, might lead him to require the same amount every day. This thought was enough to bring us to a dead halt. . . ."

There was some truth to the slaveholders' contention that white factory hands in the North were forced to work harder than black field hands in the South. Frederick Law Olmstead, who traveled widely through the Southern states in the 1850's, observed that the slaves went through the motions of labor without putting any strength into it, and he speculated that perhaps they kept their powers in reserve for the nights when their time was their own. Olmstead gave this description of a work gang on a South Carolina plantation:

"The overseer rode about among them, on a horse, carrying in his hand a raw-hide whip, constantly directing and encouraging them; but . . . as often as he visited one end of the line of operations, the hands at the other end would discontinue their labors until he turned to ride towards them again."

The workers developed a variety of simple, energy-conserving tricks, such as concealing rocks at the bottom of their cotton baskets to meet the quota at weighing-in time, but the favorite was playing sick. There was one man on a Mississippi plantation, the husband of a cook, who got out of doing work by persuading his master that he was nearly blind. No sooner did he get some land of his own after the Civil War than he became one of the best farmers in the county. A worker on a South Carolina plantation complained of rheumatism during the week, but on Sundays he surreptitiously rowed fifteen miles to a market to do a bit of trading for his personal profit. Another man seemed so lazy that his owner gave him a chance to work out his freedom just to get rid of him; given this incentive, he set vigorously to work and was soon free.

A more direct expression of resistance to slavery and all that it meant was simply to run away. People fled from their plantations for various reasons—fear of punishment for some infraction of the rules; a feeling that they had been treated too harshly by their owner or overseer; a desire to rejoin their families or friends; a mere wish to avoid work.

The runaways were usually young men, under thirty, and the most popular months for their adventure were June and September, when work was hardest and travel easiest. Most often they went off alone or in pairs, and did not go very far or stay away for very long. They rarely took anything with them besides the clothes on their backs, but now and then one managed to make off with a remarkable assortment of

Fugitives arriving at the Coffin farm in Indiana, a busy station on the Underground Railroad. From a painting by C. T. Webber

merchandise. In 1824, a Mississippi man named Isaac ran away wearing a fur hat, a ruffled shirt, a snuff-colored coat, a red and white striped vest, a pair of yellow pantaloons, and new boots with brass heels, and carrying several hundred dollars' worth of his former master's goods.

Not infrequently a slave who had been hired out by his owner for a set period would stay away until the hiring period was over, whereupon he would return—to a probable whipping. But often the owner, in the words of one observer, "glad to find his property safe and that it has not died in the swamp, or gone to Canada, forgets to punish him, and immediately sends him for another year to a new master."

For Virginia slaves, the large swampy areas were favorite hiding places, and many stayed there for months. One owner reported that he could often see the fires on which runaways cooked the sheep, pigs, calves, and fowl they captured or stole. If they grew hungry or cold, they could usually slip back to the plantation in the knowledge that a fellow slave would assist them with some corn or a night's shelter. Numbers of runaways in the forests, mountains, and swamps of the South formed their own communities, which were called "maroons."

Some young men ran off so many times that they were forced to work in irons. A repeated offender on a Louisiana plantation was put in an iron halter with a bell attached, to make recapture easier. Still, there were always some who refused to be discouraged, who refused to exist as slaves: a woman in North Carolina fled from her plantation no less than fifteen times. And there were some who chose death over bondage: a fugitive from a Louisiana plantation was tracked down, with the help of dogs, to a Mississippi River flatboat where he had been working as a free Negro. Armed with a club and a pistol, he stood on a large raft and threatened to kill anyone who attempted to lay hands on him. His pursuers shot him, but, in the words of an eyewitness, "so determined was he not to be captured that when an effort was made to rescue him from drowning, he made battle with his club, and sunk waving his weapon in angry defiance."

A man who fled to Virginia's Dismal Swamp told this story of a dramatic and fatal encounter there:

"I saw wid my own eyes when dey shot Jacob. Dat is too bad to 'member. God will not forget it, never, I bet ye. Six white men comed upon him afore he knowed nothin' at all 'bout it most. Jist de first ting Jacob seed was his old Master, Simon Simms, of Suffolk, Virginny, standing right afore him. Dem ar men —all on em—had a gun apiece, an' dey every one of dem pointed right straight to de head of poor Jacob. He felt scared most to def. Old Simms hollered out to him—'Jake! You run a step, you nigger, and I'll blow yer brains out!' Jacob didn't know for de life on him what to do. Six guns wid number two shot aimed at your head isn't nothin', I tell ye. Takes brave man to stand dat, 'cordin' to my reck'nin'. Jacob lift up his feet to run. Mercy on him! De Master and one ob de men levelled dar guns, and dar guns levelled poor Jacob."

Attempts to escape permanently, beyond nearby woods and swamps, north to freedom, were much more hazardous, involving miles and miles of travel by night through strange country. Indeed, fleeing north from the Deep South was a nearly impossible undertaking. Frederick Douglass described the fears that he and his fellow plotters felt when they were planning their escape even from the border state of Maryland:

"The case, sometimes to our excited visions, stood thus: At every gate through which we had to pass, we saw a watchman; at every ferry, a guard; on every bridge, a sentinel; and in every wood, a patrol or a slave hunter. . . . No man can tell the intense agony which is felt by the slave when wavering on the point of making his escape."

Yet, despite enormous hardships and countless failures, men like Douglass succeeded. Year after year hundreds fled. As one of the escapees wrote afterwards to his former master, with whom he had been on quite amiable terms: ". . . What can a man do who has his hands bound and his feet fettered? He will certainly try to get them loosened in any way that he may think the most advisable."

Some runaways had help from "conductors" along the famous Underground Railroad—like Harriet Tubman, who devoted much of her life after her own escape from the eastern shore of Maryland to leading other Negroes to freedom. The Underground Railroad, of course, was not a railroad and it was not underground: it consisted of a series of hiding places, especially in Ohio and Pennsylvania, where escapees on their way to Canada could find food and shelter. As Edward Hicks, who fled from Virginia to Canada, remarked: "We have got some good white friends in the United States. If it had not been for them, I would not have got here."

Numbers of escapees were sent back south under the provisions of the Fugitive Slave Law, which provided for the return of those who had fled from one state to another, a particularly bitter postscript to a taste of freedom. As might have been expected, there was little disposition to return voluntarily. After twenty years of freedom, devoted to piloting hundreds of people into Canada, the Reverend J. W. Loguen received a letter from his former mistress in Tennessee demanding that he return. He wrote back:

"You say you have offers to buy me and that you

# CAUTION!!

# COLORED PEOPLE

## OF BOSTON, ONE & ALL,

You are hereby respectfully CAUTIONED and advised, to avoid conversing with the

# Watchmen and Police Officers of Boston,

For since the recent ORDER OF THE MAYOR & ALDERMEN, they are empowered to act as

# KIDNAPPERS

## AND

# Slave Catchers,

And they have already been actually employed in KIDNAPPING, CATCHING, AND KEEPING SLAVES. Therefore, if you value your LIBERTY, and the *Welfare of the Fugitives* among you, *Shun* them in every possible manner, as so many *HOUNDS* on the track of the most unfortunate of your race.

# Keep a Sharp Look Out for KIDNAPPERS, and have TOP EYE open.

*APRIL 24, 1851.*

This placard was posted by the Vigilance Committee of Boston as a warning to fugitive slaves

shall sell me if I do not send you $1,000, and in the same breath and almost in the same sentence, you say, 'You know we raised you as we did our own children.' Woman, did you raise your own children for the market? Did you raise them for the whipping post? Did you raise them to be driven off, bound to a coffle in chains? Where are my poor bleeding brothers and sisters? Can you tell? Who was it that sent them off into sugar and cotton fields, to be kicked and cuffed and whipped, and to groan and die; and where no kin can hear their groans, or attend and sympathize at their dying bed, or follow in their funeral?"

Another man, invited to return to his former master's plantation after the Civil War, replied that he would consider the invitation if the plantation owner would just send him the sum of $11,680 back pay for his thirty-two years of past service. Plus interest.

It was a special source of mystification to slaveholders that those very servants whom they had treated best should sometimes run off—a phenomenon on which Frederick Douglass shed some light:

"Beat and cuff your slave, keep him hungry and spiritless, and he will follow the chain of his master like a dog; but feed and clothe him well—work him moderately, surround him with physical comfort—and dreams of freedom intrude. Give him a *bad* master and he aspires to a *good* master; give him a good master, and he wishes to become his *own* master."

Although, as we have noted, black men tended to conceal their inmost longings from whites, occasionally their dreams of freedom burst through. In Louisiana, the journalist Frederick Law Olmstead got into conversation with a house servant who had been raised in Virginia and shipped south when he was thirteen. Olmstead asked him what he would do if he was free, and he replied with emotion:

"If I was free, massa; if I was free, I would—well, sar, de fus thing I would do, if I was free, I would go to work for a year and get some money for myself—den—den—den, massa, dis is what I do—I buy me, fus place, a little house, and little lot land, and den—no, den—den —I would go to old Virginny, and see my old mudder. Yes, sar, I would like to do dat fus thing; den, when I com back de fus thing I'd do, I'd get me a wife; den, I'd take her to my house, and I would live with her dar; and I would raise things in my garden, and take 'em to New Orleans, and sell 'em dar, in de market. Dat's de way I would live, if I was free."

The dream of freedom played a part in the scores of slave conspiracies, attacks on overseers and owners, and even attempted poisonings in the South, particularly as the national debate over slavery moved toward its bloody climax. The great majority of the conspiracies were small, involving but a handful of people, and doomed to failure. Yet they were an irrepressible expression of black discontent and aspiration. They demonstrated, too, that there were highly gifted black men who did not at all fit into the white Southerner's picture of the ideal Negro. They were capable of secretly organizing disciplined black forces —a remarkable feat under the restrictions imposed by the slave system—and were ready to give their lives to their cause.

Insurrections occurred in a variety of circumstances. In 1730, ninety-six Africans on a slave ship six days out of the coast of Guinea got loose of their chains, took over the ship, and sailed back to Africa. About a hundred years later, a group of slaves aboard the *Lafayette*, which was taking them from Norfolk to New Orleans, revolted, their intention being to redirect the ship to Santo Domingo, where they would be free; but their effort was put down. In 1826, on a ship bound from Baltimore to Georgia, twenty-nine slaves rose up, threw the captain and his mate overboard, and set out for Haiti; they were recaptured and wound up in New York, where, evidently, they escaped or were allowed to go free.

There were also attempted escapes from the slave coffles that moved south overland. For example, on one such coffle, made up of ninety men, women, and children, heading south from Maryland in August 1829, two of the men began what appeared to be a fight. It was a ruse, part of an escape plan. Two of the three white guards who rushed in to separate them were killed and a third was injured. The slaves escaped but were soon recaptured and five of the leaders were hung. According to a contemporary report, one of the condemned men went to his death with the cry: "Death—death at any time in preference to slavery!"

Reports of such incidents fed the fears of planters, outnumbered as they were by Negroes on their own plantations, and sometimes they went on witchhunts, which resembled those in Massachusetts in colonial days. An anti-slavery minister has left us a description of how rumor led to panic, which led to brutal punishment:

"Somebody starts a report that 'the niggers are going to rise.' Messrs. Scared-to-death & Co. take up a servant Bob, strip off his shirt, make him 'hug' a tree, and then tie him in that position.

"Mr. Stonyhead steps forward: 'Did you hear Bill Black say that the niggers were going to rise and kill the whites?'

" 'No, sir.'

" 'You lie, you rascal!' Click! Click! Click! goes the cowhide; the blood flows and the boy writhes in agony at every stroke. 'Now confess, you dog.'

" 'O yes, Massa! O, let me down, Massa, and I will confess. Bill did say to me that the niggers were going to rise.'

"Away they go after Bill. He is caught, and a rope is adjusted to his neck. In vain he protests his innocence;

he is hung up to the nearest tree just like a dog, with no semblance of trial."

Despite merciless suppression, the spirit that moved the rebellious slaves, whose leaders were typically both intelligent and highly skilled, kept flaring up. Southern observers remarked on the manner in which captured leaders went to their deaths; they seemed quite calm and showed neither fear nor regret.

An insight into the power of their resolve is provided by an extraordinary interview that a white minister had with a South Carolina man named Isaac who was awaiting execution for his role in an aborted insurrection. The minister, a friend of Isaac's, asked him how it was that he had been prepared to murder his master, whom he said he loved. Isaac replied:

"Master, I was a slave. My wife and children were slaves. If equal with others before God they should be equal before men. I saw my young masters learning, holding what they made and making what they could. But, master, my race could make nothing, holding nothing. What they did they did for others, not for themselves. And they had to do it, whether they wished it or not; for they were slaves. Master, this is not loving our neighbor or doing to others as we would have them do to us. I know there was and could be no help for mine, for wife or children, for my race, except we were free; and as the whites would not let this be, and as God told me he could only help those who helped themselves, I preached freedom to the slaves, and bid them strike for it like men."

The leadership of exceptional men like the obscure Isaac was a major generating force in the slave conspiracies. The conspiracies could not have developed as extensively as a few of them did, however, without a sense of solidarity among the field hands. Whereas house servants lived in close and often affectionate contact with whites, the laborers who shared the plantation's slave quarters were off by themselves, their lives and fates tied to each other. And it was in the slave quarters that the leaders found followers.

Three major conspiracies stand out in the history of American slavery. The first, which occurred near Richmond, Virginia, in 1800, was led by a big, twenty-four-year-old man named Gabriel Prosser. During the spring of the year, hundreds of the area's slaves were drawn into the plan, accumulating home-made swords and bayonets as well as clubs, scythes, and a few guns. The uprising was set for August 30, but word leaked out. Two slaves, Tom and Pharaoh, told their owner of the plot, and Virginia's Governor James Monroe (later to be President of the United States) alerted the state militia. It rained very heavily on August 30, and the downpour made it impossible for the assembled rebels—about a thousand of them—to cross a bridge into Richmond. They disbanded, and the authorities hunted down the leaders.

One eyewitness to part of the affair, John Randolph, commented: "The accused have exhibited a spirit which, if it becomes general, must deluge the country in blood. They manifested a sense of their rights, and contempt of danger, and a thirst for revenge which portend the most unhappy consequences."

About thirty-five of the conspirators were hung, including Gabriel, who escaped but was captured in Norfolk after being recognized by two Negroes. A Richmond man who saw some of the rebels hanged wrote: "Of those who have been executed, no one has betrayed his cause. They have uniformly met death with fortitude." This fortitude comes through strongly in the reported answer of one of the captured men to the inquisitors at his trial:

"I have nothing more to offer than what General Washington would have had to offer, had he been taken by the British officers and put to trial by them. I have ventured my life in endeavoring to obtain the liberty of my countrymen, and am a willing sacrifice to their cause; and I beg, as a favor, that I may be immediately led to execution."

In Charleston, South Carolina, in 1822, a plot arose led by Denmark Vesey, a free Negro in his fifties whose children were still slaves. The uprising, during which thousands of men equipped with bayonets and daggers were supposed to converge on Charleston along five separate routes, put the city to the torch, and annihilate the white population, was planned for a Sunday in July, when a large number of whites would be away at resorts. Despite great care, extending over many months, in organizing the rebels (one of Vesey's lieutenants warned an agent not to mention the plot "to those waiting men who receive presents of old coats, etc. from their masters, or they'll betray us . . ."), a few Negroes informed and the plan was quashed.

Between June 18 and August 9, thirty-seven of the plotters, including Denmark Vesey himself, were hanged. The ringleaders were drawn through the streets of Charleston in carts, each seated on the coffin that would contain his body. Most of them followed the admonition of one leader to "die silent, as you shall see me do." Their bodies were left hanging in a row as a warning to the area's slaves, and a strict 9 p.m. curfew for Negroes was put into effect.

The most famous and the bloodiest of the slave conspiracies took place in 1831 in Southampton County, Virginia. It was led by a gifted thirty-year-old man named Nat Turner, a preacher to the slaves, who seems to have been impelled by what he believed was a heavenly command to free his people. A white man wrote of him:

# RESISTANCE

"It is notorious, that he was never known to have a dollar in his life; to swear an oath, or drink a drop of spirits. As to his ignorance, he certainly never had the advantages of education, but he can read and write (it was taught him by his parents), and for natural intelligence and quickness of apprehension is surpassed by few men I have ever seen."

Between August 21 and August 24, Turner's band, which grew to more than sixty men, made its way from house to house with the object of carrying "terror and devastation wherever we went." Before they were done, they had killed between fifty and sixty whites—men, women, and children. The rebels were finally defeated by a much superior force, and scores of Negroes in the county fell at the hands of frightened and vengeful whites. Nat Turner himself was not caught until the end of October; he was promptly tried, found guilty, and hung, leaving behind him one of the most remarkable documents in the history of slavery—*The Confessions of Nat Turner*.

Nat Turner's revolt shocked the South and brought on a multitude of repressive measures. A Negro who was in Virginia at the time recalled: "Slaves were whipped, hung and cut down with swords in the streets, if found away from their quarters after dark."

Yet in the coming years the cry for freedom would resound through the country—in the powerful protests of the Northern abolitionists, white and black; in the consciences of hundreds of thousands of Americans; in the spirits of the slaves themselves. In South Carolina they sang:

*Arise! Arise! Shake off your chains.*
*Your cause is just, so Heaven ordains.*
*To you shall Freedom be proclaimed.*
*To you shall Freedom be proclaimed.*

# EPILOGUE

# *FREEDOM*

Years after the Civil War, an old woman thought back to her hour of freedom:

"When Old Master comes down in the cotton patch to tell us 'bout being free, he say, 'I hates to tell you, but I knows I's got to—you is free, just as free as me or anybody else what's white.' We didn't hardly know what he means. We just sort of huddle round together like scared rabbits, but after we knowed what he mean, didn't many of us go, 'cause we didn't know where to of went."

Freedom, as black people soon learned, was no simple gift; it had to be won, and then won again and again. Along with great promise, it brought new responsibilities for which slavery was a poor preparation.

It called for knowledge and experience and courage in its exercise. It required not only a terrible Civil War and a noble Emancipation Proclamation, but a revolution in the entire way of life of the South, which met obstructions from all sides. Many years after the war, a "freedman" in the South said:

"It seems like the white people can't git over us being free, and they do everything to hold us down all the time. We don't git no schools for a long time. . . . And we can't go round where they have the voting, unless we want to catch a whipping some night, and we have to just keep on bowing and scraping when we are round white folks like we did when we was slaves. They had us down and they kept us down."

A hundred years ago, black people sang:

> *I'm so glad I got free at las',*
> *Free at las', free at las'—*
> *Slavery's chains done broke at las',*
> *Broke at las', broke at las'!*

But today, more than a century after the Emancipation Proclamation, despite long strides, the black man's struggle to shake off the oppressive heritage of slavery is far from ended.

# SELECTED BIBLIOGRAPHY

The following are a few works, of the many on slavery in America, that are likely to be of particular interest to young people:

*Black Cargoes,* by Daniel P. Mannix and Malcolm Cowley, 1962
> A highly readable history of the African slave trade.

*The Cotton Kingdom,* by Frederick Law Olmstead, 1861
> A report on life in the Slave States by a clear-sighted journalist.

*Journal of a Residence on a Georgian Plantation,* by Frances (Fanny) Anne Kemble, 1864
> A sensitive young English actress's encounter with slavery on her husband's plantation.

*Lay My Burden Down,* edited by B. A. Botkin, 1945
> The often moving recollections of former slaves.

# BLACK BONDAGE

*Narrative of My Experience in Slavery,* by Frederick Douglass, 1845
> The life and reflections of the great American Negro leader.

*Out of the Mouths of Ex-Slaves,* edited by John B. Cade. *Journal of Negro History,* Volume 20
> Memories of slavery.

*The Refugee,* edited by Benjamin Drew, 1856
> The personal experiences of some of those who succeeded in escaping from bondage.

*The Roving Editor,* by James Redpath, 1859
> A Northern journalist's illuminating conversations with slaves and slaveholders.

*Truth Stranger than Fiction,* by Josiah Henson, 1858
> The autobiography of the man who is said to have served as the prototype for Uncle Tom in Harriet Beecher Stowe's *Uncle Tom's Cabin.*

*Twelve Years a Slave,* by Solomon Northup, 1854
> The informative, exciting, and often witty story of a talented free Negro who was kidnapped from New York and sold into slavery into Louisiana.

# INDEX

Anderson, Robert, 121

*Black Cargoes,* 14
Brown, Henry "Box," 98

Civil War, 4, 63, 83, 90, 113, 120, 124, 133, 143-144
Clothing, 29-30
*Confessions of Nat Turner,* 141
Conspiracies, 138-142
Cowley, Malcolm, 14

Diet, 23-24
Disease, 31-33
Douglass, Frederick, 3, 41, 47, 51, 53, 66-69, 72, 77-78, 88, 94, 115, 123, 129, 133
Durgin and Bailey's shipyard, 54

Education, 50-55

Emancipation, 4, 18, 37, 114, 144
Emancipation Proclamation, 4, 144
English Royal Africa Company, 15
Epps (slaveholder), 24
Escape, 124-136

Family, see marriage and family
Field work, 18-22
Freeman (slaveholder), 105-107
Fugitive Slave Law, 130

Gadsden, General James, 96

Hamptons (slaveholders), 37
Health, 31-33
Henson, Josiah, 26, 43, 98-101, 119, 121

# INDEX

Hicks, Edward, 130
Holidays, 47-48
House servants, 17, 34-38
Hughes, Louis, 94

Insurrections, 135-138

Kemble, Francis (Fanny) Anne,
   33, 38, 44, 52, 87, 93, 117

*Lafayette* (slave ship), 135
Law and the slave, 76-78
Leisure, see play and leisure
Lincoln, Abraham, 4, 114
Living quarters, 25-29
Lloyd, Colonel (slaveholder),
   115-116
Loguen, Rev. J. W., 130

Mannix, Daniel P., 14
Marriage and family, 85-112
Mix, Amanda, 102
Monroe, James, 138

Northup, Solomon, 25, 48, 64,
   70, 73, 104

Olmstead, Frederick Law, 83,
   123, 134

Patrols, 79-80, 83
*Peculiar Institution, The*, 90
Pimlico (plantation), 95-96
Play and leisure, 42-62

Plummer (overseer), 66-67
Prosser, Gabriel, 138-139
Punishment, 63-84

Randolph, John, 139
Reed, Colonel (slaveholder), 34
Religion, 55-63
Riley, Isaac, 98-101

Sale of slaves, 8, 97, 102-107
Schooling, 49-55
Ships, slave, 8-16, 135
Simms, Simon, 128
Simpkins, Mary, 103
Stampp, Kenneth, 90, 119
Stowe, Harriet Beecher, 26
Sugar House, 70

Taylor (slaveholder), 76
Tubman, Harriet, 130
Turner, Nat, 140-141

*Uncle Tom's Cabin*, 26
Underground Railroad, 130
Union Army, 114, 120

Vesey, Denmark, 139-140

Washington, Booker T., 30, 50,
   113
Washington, George, 139
Weddings, 88-90
Woodson, Carter, 72
Woodson, Dr. Carter, 72